The Emotion Trap

SIRI HELLE

The Emotion Trap

**WHY NEGATIVE FEELINGS
HOLD YOU BACK AND HOW
SMALL CHANGES CAN
SET YOU FREE**

Translated by A. A. Prime

Lagom

First published in the UK by Lagom
An imprint of The Zaffre Publishing Group
A Bonnier Books UK company
4th Floor, Victoria House,
Bloomsbury Square,
London, WC1B 4DA

Owned by Bonnier Books
Sveavägen 56, Stockholm, Sweden

Trade Paperback – 9781788709316
Ebook – 9781788709309
Audio – 9781788709293

A CIP catalogue of this book is available from the British Library.

Designed by Envy Design Ltd
Printed and bound by Clays Ltd, Elcograf S.p.A.

1 3 5 7 9 10 8 6 4 2

Every reasonable effort has been made to trace copyright holders of material
reproduced in this book, but if any have been inadvertently overlooked the
publishers would be glad to hear from them.

Lagom is an imprint of Bonnier Books UK
www.bonnierbooks.co.uk

All examples in this book are inspired by real cases but details have been changed to protect anonymity. My hope is that many of you will recognise yourselves in these descriptions – at the end of the day, we aren't all that different from our fellow human beings.

'Action seems to follow feeling, but really action and feeling go together; and by regulating the action, which is under the more direct control of the will, we can indirectly regulate the feeling, which is not.'
WILLIAM JAMES, PSYCHOLOGIST (1922)

'Move your ass and your mind will follow.'
FRANK MÖLLER, ELECTROPUNK ARTIST (2006)

CONTENTS

Introduction

Waiting in the wings, I stared as though hypnotised at 'TED' spelled out in red letters on stage. I needed the toilet. As always when I'm nervous, I had been drinking copious amounts of water to combat my dry mouth and had become stuck in an endless loop of drinking and running to the ladies'.

But it was too late to go again. It was almost my turn.

It was all so surreal. Only three years earlier, I had been shuffling between psychology lectures like a zombie. To say I was shy would be an understatement – sometimes I stuttered when making small talk with my classmates. I had crumpled up my childhood dream of becoming a writer and tossed it in the bin along with several failed novel attempts.

But now I was a writer, and more besides. I was soon to follow up the non-fiction book I had co-authored, which was the basis for the TEDx talk I was about to give, with my debut novel the following spring. I hadn't even graduated yet but I had already made my radio debut to an audience of 400,000 and written for Sweden's largest daily newspaper.

It was like magic. Everything that had once held me back – lack of motivation, self-doubt, worry and anxiety – was no longer an issue. These problems hadn't vanished completely (my constant need to pee being a telltale sign) but they were no longer at the wheel. I was in the driver's seat of my own life.

Except it absolutely was not magic. Far from it! It all came from one single, simple principle that I had learned in my psychology degree. The same approach used in CBT to treat depression, overcome phobias and manage severe anxiety.

I found myself asking the same question as countless clients have asked following successful treatment: why doesn't everyone learn about this?

'Please give a warm welcome for our next speaker: Siri Helle!'

You can give a TEDx talk despite nerves.

I let out a deep breath, smiled and stepped on stage.

A Rose by Any Other Name

Don't get me wrong, emotions are amazing. They can make you strong and selfless. They can give you the courage to stand up for what you believe in and the motivation to meet life's challenges head on.

But they can also sabotage you. Massively. Emotions can make you act impulsively, illogically or downright self-destructively. We all have our own unique ways of tripping ourselves up. You might say that your biggest problem is procrastination, anxiety, low self-esteem, overthinking . . . it goes by many names. I call it 'the emotion trap' and I am going to teach you how to overcome it.

The **emotion trap** is when you act on your emotions because it feels right at the time, even though it only makes things worse in the long run. Do you recognise any of these classic emotion traps in your own life?

- You procrastinate by scrolling on your phone, snacking or fiddling instead of getting your teeth into the task you're supposed to be doing.

- You skip a workout session because curling up on the sofa is so much more appealing.

- You dream about all the things you would do if only you had better self-esteem or more motivation – but you never get around to doing any of them.

- You let your fears stand in the way of your dreams.

- You become paralysed with performance anxiety because you set impossibly high expectations for yourself – much higher than you would for anyone else.

- You're so busy thinking about tough things that have happened or horrible things that might happen that you find it difficult to enjoy the present moment.

- You stay in a soul-destroying job or a loveless relationship because deep down you don't feel like you deserve any better.

- You fritter away money on alcohol, gambling or shopping to numb difficult feelings.

- You spend hours googling symptoms and convince yourself that you're suffering from extremely rare but life-threatening illnesses.

- You cry over the jumper your ex left behind and listen to 'your songs', even though you know you need to move on.

- You chase validation in the form of social media likes and flashy gadgets, but still feel that no one has really seen you.

- You work like a dog to make time to relax later. Strangely enough, the time to relax never seems to come.

- You spend hours anxiously brooding on why something has happened to you – rather than trying to do something about the situation.

- You convince yourself that you don't care about something. Whereas your behaviour proves time and time again that you care a lot.

- You become fixated on jealous fantasies that threaten to destroy your relationship in real life.

- You cancel plans because you're in a bad mood. Even though moping around at home, re-watching old TV shows and stewing over how crappy you feel is hardly going to make you feel better.

I'm sure you can come up with any number of examples of occasions when it feels like your emotions are making your decisions for you. The sneaky thing about emotion traps is that they often feel right at the time. Acting on your impulses gives you a temporary sense of relief and comfort. It's only afterwards, when you're forced to deal with the consequences of your actions, that you realise your mistake.

Emotion traps don't solve your problems. On the contrary, after you've fallen at a particular hurdle once, you're more likely to repeat the same mistake over and over. Then, as the problem worsens so too do the unpleasant feelings associated with it. If you're really unlucky, you might get stuck in a downward spiral that's difficult to escape.

If you're someone who becomes trapped in these sorts of self-destructive patterns, you are not alone. By the time you've finished this book, you will understand why you keep falling into the same traps and how to break free. You will have the tools to reclaim your power and change your behaviour in everyday life.

This might sound like a rather grandiose promise. From the outside, all these problems look very different, but on the inside, they are all based on the same psychological mechanisms.

You might think of feelings as something abstract and superfluous – maybe you associate the idea of emotions with romantic comedies and herbal tea – but, in fact, they are an indispensable biological mechanism. Your impulses are emotional responses programmed by evolution and your life experiences. They are there to ensure your survival. Most of the time, this programming functions excellently, but sometimes, bugs arise and these are what I call emotion traps.

The good news is that decades of psychological research have shown that it is possible to 'hack' this system. You can reprogramme yourself by using a psychological method that you should have been taught years ago.

I call it the **behaviour principle**. By acting in line with the feeling you want to achieve (rather than the feeling you already have) you can break established patterns. A single subtle but conscious change in behaviour can kick-start a psychological feedback loop that fundamentally alters your thoughts and feelings. If you behave calmly, your stress levels will drop. If you act bravely, your fear will diminish. You turn the negative spiral into a positive one and take control of your life. Instead of struggling with emotions and ingrained thought patterns, you take a shortcut.

On the surface, this might sound like an inspirational Instagram quote. Fake it till you make it. But there are some important differences between the behaviour principle and common clichés, which we will discuss soon. This isn't about ignoring, forbidding or denying difficult feelings. Neither is it a method that requires particular drive or mental strength. It's a tool for gradually and compassionately rising to meet life's challenges, for inviting new thoughts and feelings into everyday life and noticing that they accept the invitation more often than you might think.

This isn't something I made up myself (though I sometimes like to daydream that I did). I spent half my youth poring over self-help books and I was shocked at how many 'old truths' my psychology degree swept away in favour of scientifically proven methods. As a clinical psychologist, I participated in countless CBT treatments and conveyed the same principles to six clients a day. After a few years, I found myself wondering if there wasn't a more efficient way to spread the message.

I've worked in private practice, primary care and at a specialist clinic for severe anxiety and depression. The latter is for seriously ill people who have tried at least two treatments before without sufficient results. Yet I kept hearing the same thing over and over again: 'Why hasn't anyone told me this before?'

Let me tell you this now, so we don't have to meet in therapy in ten years' time. A decade from now, I hope that you're travelling the world, living happily with the love of your life, thriving in your dream job or whatever else it is that you desire, but which the emotion trap is preventing you from doing today.

If you're suffering from really serious problems then put down this book and find someone you can talk to – preferably a doctor or psychologist. But if, like me, you struggle with normal levels of anxiety, stress or lack of motivation, I have some important lessons for you. Of course, I cannot know what emotions you're dealing with. I'm a psychologist, not a mind reader (although people confuse the two surprisingly often). Therefore, in this book, I will go through the most common challenges: self-esteem, joy, motivation, anxiety and stress. Ultimately, you're holding a manual for a somewhat happier, somewhat more efficient life.

Since you're far from alone in struggling with the emotion trap, you will also receive advice on how to support friends who repeatedly sabotage themselves. You can provide valuable support for someone else to make a change.

But before we get into the nitty-gritty of the emotion trap and behaviour principle, let's go back to basics. You're going to need a brief introductory course in human psychology.

A Crash Course in Psychology

Human psychology is infinitely complicated, but let's not make it harder than it needs to be. You'll be surprised how far you can get by boiling it down to three simple ingredients: thoughts, feelings and behaviours.

Thoughts – don't believe everything you think

We like to believe that our thoughts are objective descriptions of reality. Unfortunately, there is a huge amount of psychological research to suggest the contrary. Take a look at the following examples of studies:

- Nearly half of all participants in a British study remembered seeing footage of the car crash that killed Princess Diana on television. The problem? No such footage was ever broadcast.

- Ninety-seven per cent of all Swedish motorists claim to be average or above-average drivers.

- Participants were given a film to watch of a teacher either acting in a warm and friendly or cold and unpleasant manner. When the teacher was kind, his French accent and appearance were perceived as attractive; when he was unpleasant, they were considered off-putting.

Thoughts are the conscious processes that occur in your head every day, often in the form of words or mental images.

As a human being, you are equipped with the ability to think abstractly. You can also make mental jumps between past, present and future. These are amazing abilities that allow you to plan, imagine and solve problems.

Unfortunately, these superpowers come at a cost. They've done more than just enable humanity to build complex societies, complete with frozen pizzas and self-driving cars. They've also created the conditions for you to be sitting in the sunshine, enjoying a cup of coffee – and feeling stressed about a presentation you have to give on Thursday.

The human brain is not a flawless computer program that scans its surroundings, processes the data and calculates the most logical conclusion. The common biases mentioned above aren't the preserve of Brits and Swedish motorists. Memories change and are 'rewritten' every time you recall them ('I swear, the fish weighed at least five kilos!'). An idiotic idea can sound brilliant when coming from someone you admire. Your mood affects how you interpret information, which is why companies try to butter you up with free gifts in an attempt to win your loyalty.

Thoughts provide important information about the world, but you shouldn't believe everything you think. Remember this – it's a lesson that will be important later on.

Feelings – providing signals to you and those around you

Feelings are internal states. They arise as reactions to changes in your environment or inside yourself. Just like thoughts, feelings fulfil various functions.

- **Signals to yourself.** Feelings give almost instantaneous information about your experience of any given situation. For example, fear is a sign that you might be in danger and shame is a sign that you've broken a social norm.

- **Communication with others.** The way you express your emotions communicates what's going on inside your head to the people around you. This is incredibly useful for pack animals like human beings. If someone is scowling and looks like they're on the war path, then you try not to get in their way.

- **Heightened readiness for action.** When you're frightened you will jump at the smallest sound and when you're curious you will find the courage to explore. Feelings make you react to situations faster and more appropriately than if you had to stop to analyse what was going on intellectually.

Even though feelings fulfil many essential functions, they're not always well calibrated. A horror film can absolutely terrify you even though you're sitting in perfect safety with a bowl of popcorn.

Feelings give important signals but they're no oracle.

You can feel several things at the same time and these feelings can be contradictory. If a friend of yours wins the lottery, it's natural to be both happy and envious, even if there is a cultural expectation to only express happiness. Your culture defines social norms around which feelings you're expected to display and how and when to do so. Of course, these norms are changing all the time. For example, it's becoming more acceptable to say that you're not okay.

It takes a lot of practice to get good at defining your feelings. You are shaped by your upbringing and the ways in which the people around you mirror your emotional reactions. 'You poor thing! Does it hurt?' you might say to a child who has fallen over and is crying. If, on the other hand, you were taught that emotions are silly and need to be kept under control, you may find it difficult to determine how you genuinely feel in different situations as an adult.

This can cause problems if, for example, you confuse tiredness after a long day with anger that someone has left dirty dishes on the counter. It can also cause you to push beyond your limits and take on more even when your body is trying to warn you that you're exhausted.

You can practise emotional self-awareness by noticing your feelings and putting them into words. A common challenge is being able to distinguish feelings from thoughts. Feelings can often be labelled with a single word, such as 'angry', 'disappointed' or 'restless'. Thus, 'I feel like an idiot' is not a feeling but a thought that might accompany the feeling of shame.

Behaviours – you're always doing something

Last but not least, we've got **behaviours**, or actions. Behaviours can be small and subtle, like clenching your fists or avoiding eye contact. Or they can be whole processes, such as going to a party or quitting your job.

Subtle behaviours are easy to overlook, even though they play a significant role in your life and relationships. One example I have come across in therapy is people who feel left out and bored when hanging out with their friends. This might be a consequence of them sitting back and wondering what's wrong with them instead of participating in conversations and guiding them to topics that interest them.

You're always doing something. Even when you say you're 'doing nothing', you're still engaging in some sort of behaviour, such as lying in bed and staring at the ceiling (and giving your thoughts free rein to keep replaying that embarrassing memory of nobody laughing at that joke you told at lunch).

Therefore, the most effective way to stop doing something is often to start doing something else. Preferably a behaviour that has the same aim as the problematic behaviour but which is better for you in the long run. For example, many people want to cut down on their screen time but find it difficult to keep their fingers off their mobile phone when they are restless or bored. Instead of getting stuck in a loop of self-criticism, it's probably better to fix the restlessness itself – for example, by arranging to see friends or getting a hobby.

The Psychological Triangle

These three building blocks – thoughts, feelings and behaviours – are connected and affect each other. Let's call this the **psychological triangle**. If you change one corner of the triangle, the other two are affected. This might sound obvious. But when you realise the extent of this correlation, you can start to decipher even the most seemingly baffling human behaviour.

Imagine you're on a date.

Your thoughts affect your feelings. If all you think about is the mistakes you're making, you're going to feel pretty nervous and awkward.

Your thoughts affect your behaviour. Instead of asking for a second date, you might invent a reason to skulk away. If you're convinced that you're going to be rejected, you may as well spare yourself the humiliation.

Your feelings affect your thoughts. If you're attracted to your date, and maybe a little tipsy, their clumsy jokes might seem hilarious. If, on the other hand, you're cranky and grumpy after a long day at work (not to mention the disappointment of paying through the nose for a main course smaller than a canapé), then their attempts at humour might come off as irritating.

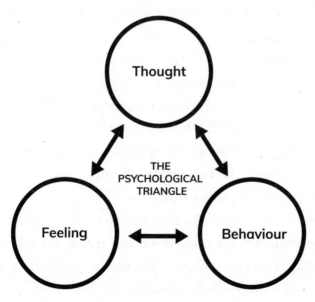

Your feelings affect your behaviour. If your heart (or any other body part) says yes, you might agree to see the other person again even if your head is telling you it's a bad idea.

Your behaviours affect your thoughts and feelings as well. Some people wonder why they never meet anyone they really like when one possible explanation is that they never direct the conversation on dates to topics that really stimulate intimacy and connection. They might be sticking to superficial small talk that makes the date feel like a job interview.

Other people seem to fall head over heels for almost anyone. This might be because they spend too much time acting out 'love behaviours', such as trying to win the other person's approval or daydreaming about the future, even though they don't really have much in common.

A consequence of the psychological triangle is that our thoughts, feelings and behaviours are constantly changing. When you're heartbroken it can feel like the pain will last forever, but as life changes and you do new things, even the most intense thoughts and feelings tend to change too. Nothing – neither happiness nor unhappiness – lasts forever.

We don't often reflect on how the three corners of the psychological triangle interact. The reactions occur more or less instinctively – which is a good thing. As previously mentioned, humankind's ability to act on feelings has been a great asset in our evolution. When we're afraid, we withdraw. When we're stressed, we work harder. This is entirely rational for an environment in which any hesitation could risk us becoming lion food.

Unfortunately, this is not a bug-free system. Think back over the last few days or so to a situation in which you acted in a way that wasn't so smart in hindsight. What feelings were influencing your behaviour at the time? Lack of sleep, stress or fear of losing something can make people impulsive. What thoughts were flying through your mind in the preceding seconds? *Better if I put it off till tomorrow*, maybe, or *they're doing that on purpose to annoy me.*

It can feel as though our reactive behaviours appear out of nowhere. But look closer and you will almost always find the underlying thoughts and feelings that explain why people act the way they do.

The Emotion Trap

This is where problems can arise.

The **emotion trap** is when you act on your emotional impulses even though it causes problems. It is when the feelings corner of the psychological triangle is allowed to dictate your behaviour, even if said behaviour is totally at odds with your long-term interests. The sneaky part is that what you're doing might feel perfectly reasonable at the time. Feelings colour your thoughts and it's all too easy to come up with explanations and excuses for why it's best to obey your impulses. You might only realise your mistake afterwards, when the initial feeling has subsided.

This might seem silly, but bear in mind that we're just apes on a rock hurtling through space. We really shouldn't expect too much of ourselves.

The human brain has evolved through a series of add-ons, not edits. The foundation of our brain is much the same as most other animal species. This epicentre of drives is commonly referred to as the limbic system (although neuropsychological research in recent decades has shown that the different processes don't really function as a unified system) and is focused on survival, avoiding danger and seeking immediate reward.

It's the relatively new part of the brain, the prefrontal cortex, that enables logical thinking. This area is activated when you need to plan, exercise self-control and make complex decisions. The prefrontal cortex can inhibit impulses from the limbic system. But if the impulses are too powerful, such as fear, they can override the logical arguments of the frontal lobes. Certain conditions such as intoxication and fatigue can also temporarily impair the function of the frontal lobes.

This is when the emotion trap can become just that – a trap. Your emotional impulses are short term;

they seek immediate reward. In the short term, it may feel good to have an angry outburst, carry on stressing over something or ignore a problem. But the underlying problem remains. It might even get worse.

If you're unlucky, the emotion trap can descend into a negative spiral. With each loop around the psychological triangle, you get further and further away from a solution. Your feelings of discomfort, frustration and exhaustion worsen. Your thoughts become increasingly negative. *I'm so useless*, you think. *That's so typical of me; I always get it wrong.*

Your behaviour can also become more and more extreme. The behaviours that might have previously alleviated your discomfort don't cut it now that your thoughts and feelings have turned up the volume. You spend more time getting distracted, double- and triple-checking that everything is okay, or lying in bed worrying about everything that might go wrong. Some people try to numb anxiety with escapism in the form of gambling, alcohol or manic partying. Even if it does provide temporary relief, sadly it usually just makes the problem worse in the long run.

The emotion trap can lead to getting stuck in patterns of behaviour that seem completely incomprehensible from the outside. Even to yourself. Why do you stay in a relationship in which you're only hurting each other? Why don't you follow your dreams? How can you harm or starve yourself when it is so obviously destructive?

The answer: because it provides a temporary sense of relief! It feels good, or at least less bad, in the short term to follow your feelings. The fact that it causes problems three minutes, three days or thirty years later is easier to ignore.

Tried, Tested and Failed Solutions

So what can we do about the emotion trap? Once you've gone around the psychological triangle a few times you start to realise that it isn't working. Something needs to change.

Many people start with the root of the pain: the feeling. However, as we've seen, the feeling itself isn't really the root of the pain after all; it is a reaction to something that has already happened. But when you're stuck in the emotion trap it oftens seems like the villain of the whole debacle.

Maybe you try to get your act together. You make an effort to change the way you feel about things through sheer willpower. You decide to stop wallowing in heartache, worry less, feel 'too blessed to be stressed'. Maybe you put a lid on your emotions and start pretending you don't feel anything at all. It goes . . . okay. Unfortunately, the human psyche doesn't have a remote control to change the emotional channel. Feelings are there whether you like it or not, along with the frustration and disappointment that you haven't been able to shake off said feelings.

Another approach is via your thoughts. All your excuses, self-doubt and justifications take place in the mind. If only you could win the debate with yourself you could break free! A whole industry has boomed around this, with books, courses and lectures all devoted to one common goal: teaching you to master your thoughts. Dedicate yourself to mental pep talks, positive visualisation or plain old good sense. Anything that can help you defeat your inner critic and talk yourself into doing the right thing. Sometimes this works. When you think rationally, you might realise that you've been overreacting or reckless. You can gain new insights that motivate change. Sometimes that's all it takes for you to succeed in breaking the vicious circle.

But if you're unlucky, the effect can be as fleeting as the thought itself. You become temporarily calm, only to think about how it might all go wrong a minute later. You feel motivated, only to find yourself back on the couch the next day with a bowl of crisps on your lap. This is often where people get stuck. Of course, our cerebral culture tells us that the brain must be the key to solving problems. Change happens from the inside out, as they say. You can repress your feelings or rationalise your thoughts. After that, it's just a case of crossing your fingers.

But there is a third alternative: you can start by changing your behaviour.

The Behaviour Principle

Acting against your impulses doesn't feel good. But it is possible. You can decide to chair a meeting at work even if you're nervous and keep doing it every week until you get used to it. You can pick up a paintbrush and get started, even if artistic inspiration eludes you. You can feel like you're not in the mood to go out to a party but put on your favourite music and do your hair anyway. It feels wrong. Your thoughts tell you it's a bad idea, that there's no point in trying. Your feelings protest and 'turn up the volume' to get you to understand.

But it works. Because here's the beautiful part: seeing as thoughts, feelings and behaviour are all connected, changing your behaviour will gradually rub off on your thoughts and feelings. By starting in the behavioural corner, you can change the dynamic of the whole psychological triangle.

By changing your behaviour, you can change your thoughts and feelings.

I call this the **behaviour principle**. By changing your behaviour, you can change your thoughts and feelings. Instead of acting in line with the feeling you're currently experiencing, act in line with the feelings you want to experience. After a while, those feelings will arise for real.

The advantage of starting in the behavioural corner is that actions – unlike thoughts and feelings – are easier to control using sheer will. It might not be much fun to clean out the basement storage room when you feel unmotivated and reluctant, but it is entirely physically possible.

There is often a certain delay before the behaviour principle produces results. If you're terrified of wasps and tend to kill them as soon as you get the chance, your fear will escalate if you sit still and let them buzz around your ears instead. It's only after you've sat still for a while and realised that they're not going to attack you that your fear eventually subsides. The changed behaviour (staying still) leads to the new thought (maybe they're not so dangerous after all) and a newfound feeling of calm, or at least diminished terror.

The wait can be excruciating. Especially if you're not familiar with the psychological triangle and don't know that the suffering is only temporary. This is one of the reasons why the behaviour principle can be difficult to discover on your own. But with a little patience, you can achieve lasting results, especially if you repeat the same behaviour several times.

The trick is to start small with a slight change in behaviour – one that takes you out of your comfort zone but is still achievable. Once you've done that, you can take another step, then another.

As your behaviour changes, your thoughts and feelings will eventually catch on. With every loop around the psychological triangle, it gets easier. The nature of thoughts changes and feelings shift. You find the courage to take bigger and bigger steps. Until one day, something that once seemed impossible now feels like the most natural thing in the world.

Of course, this doesn't work with everything. The behaviour principle is based on the assumption that your thoughts and feelings have 'got it wrong' – for example, by overestimating how upsetting, dangerous or tedious a situation actually is. If you hate aerobics with every fibre of your being, it won't matter how many sessions you do, you'll never enjoy it. If, on the other hand, you usually enjoy aerobics but just don't feel like putting on your leggings today, that feeling might change once you get up and start doing step-ups to 'Rhythm of the Night'.

The behaviour principle cannot breathe life into a dead marriage or keep you cheery through a world war, but it can help you make the best of every situation, no matter what life throws at you. This work is going on in therapy rooms all around the world, right this second. And you can be sure that I am using the behaviour principle to live my life to the fullest. Change doesn't have to happen from the inside out. It works at least as well – often better – to work from the outside in.

'Trust Your Gut'

Modern Western culture propagates the notion that you should feel a certain way in order to do certain things. It's not enough to go to work every morning just because you need the income, you're supposed to be passionate about your profession. We don't say that great art is born from a thousand tiny technical actions but from divine inspiration. To name but two examples.

When you're unsure what path to take, you're supposed to listen to your gut feeling. I imagine this is a backlash against more old-fashioned attitudes, which forced people into marriage and factories whether they felt like it or not. While it's definitely a good thing that we have moved away from this 'devotion to duty' motto, I'm not sure that 'devotion to feelings' is any better. I don't know anything about your gut – maybe it gives you wise life advice like thinking before you act and eating five portions of fruit and vegetables a day. My gut, however, thinks I should get back with my ex, despite all evidence to the contrary. It claims that popcorn is a balanced meal and that I might as well squeeze in another episode before going to sleep. On bad days, it tells me I'm worthless and would be doing the world a favour if I didn't bother getting out of bed.

Modern psychology tends to highlight personal values as a more reliable compass for everyday life. What's important to you in life? Being a good friend, your health . . . or video games? What is your biggest priority, being well rested and feeling good . . . or completing one more level?

Once you've got a good understanding of your values, you can identify and prioritise what you value in the long term – a guiding star to aim for during temporary slumps, setbacks and treacherous emotion traps.

Too Good to Be True?

At this point in therapy, some clients nod thoughtfully and say: 'That makes sense. How do we start?' If that sounds like you, then you can skip this next section.

But if you're anything like me, you're more likely to feel triggered instead. Perhaps you're already halfway through an angry email to whoever recommended you this book. You can't reduce human psychology to a silly triangle! If it was a case of 'just doing it' then you would have done it already. You've heard plenty of perky life coaches talk about this before ('fake it till you make it'), but that's easier said than done if you're dealing with childhood trauma and a family history of depression. Guess what? I absolutely agree with you. Which is why I will now go through the most common misunderstandings about the behaviour principle. Let's clear up a few questions about what the behaviour principle is and what it isn't.

It sounds too easy!

This might be the most common objection to the behaviour principle. If you've been struggling with the emotion trap for decades, you're probably expecting the solution to be just as complex as the problem. Years in therapy, at least.

And if it was a case of just doing it then you would have done it years ago. This book isn't about the Nike slogan, 'Just do it', but more *how* to do it. You can lift a car if you learn the right way to use a jack. In this book, you will learn to use the behaviour principle to reclaim control of your life, step by step.

Don't I have to understand the underlying cause?

Yes and no. If your problems have a biological cause, such as an iron deficiency, then the behaviour principle obviously isn't going to help. You need medical attention. When it comes to psychological problems, understanding the root cause can be helpful but is actually rarely necessary.

This is because psychological distress often arises as a result of three factors: genetic vulnerability, including your innate temperament and family history of mental illness; life events, i.e. your experiences in childhood and beyond; and current situation – that is, how you handle and relate to your problems here and now.

If you're looking for the reason why you feel bad, the answer is often found in a combination of all three factors. But the solution lies in the only thing you can influence: your attitude here and now.

Should I just ignore my thoughts and feelings?

Absolutely not. Thoughts and feelings provide important signals about your experience of any given situation. For example, fear is a sign of threat and anger is a sign that someone is crossing your boundaries. How you move on and handle the situation is another matter, however. Sometimes acting on your feelings is helpful; sometimes it's downright disastrous. I will teach you how to spot the difference.

Is this CBT?

This is a self-help book. Though it's based on psychological research and cognitive behavioural therapy (CBT), it mustn't be mistaken for a scientific thesis or CBT treatment. Based on the books I've read and the treatments I've worked with, I have come up with the terms 'emotion trap' and 'behaviour principle' because I think they summarise the most important lessons I've learned from CBT in a simple way. No more, no less.

But I want to be authentic!

Great, me too! The question is: authentic to what? You can love your children deeply and still find yourself shouting at them. The behaviour principle is about living authentically in line with your long-term core values, rather than temporary superficial impulses.

You don't have to fake feelings you don't have. The point is to act based on your core values and allow your feelings to be what they are.

I've tried and it doesn't work!

I can guarantee that you have tried the behaviour principle at some point and it has worked. Think of a time when you felt nervous about something but made up your mind to do it anyway – and now you can do it just fine. A shining example of the behaviour principle!

Now you are facing different challenges. You're going to have to learn to identify your obstacles, find solutions and avoid the most common pitfalls.

If you give it an honest try and still don't see any results, look into getting professional help. After all, this is only a book, not a replacement for the tailored support you receive in treatment.

Is this the solution to all my problems?

Sorry, but feeling bad sometimes is a fact of life. Sickness, disappointment, financial worries . . . Life happens and there is no vaccine for suffering. The behaviour principle is a tool to prevent unpleasant feelings from being more influential or enduring than they need to be.

But I'm happy with my life the way it is – I just want to change how I feel about it.

A lot of people wish they could find a solution that allows them to stay in their old habits but just feel differently. There's one method to achieve this and its name is drugs. Not something I recommend.

Change is hard work. It feels safer to go with what you know but if you get stuck in an uncomfortable situation, change becomes necessary.

We are going to focus on small but powerful changes in behaviour that feel achievable. Sometimes, a few tiny adjustments are all it takes to bring about life-altering results. And who knows – maybe your attitude will change once you feel that previously impossible dreams are now within reach.

STOP

The behaviour principle is a great tool. It can help you master problematic feelings from stage fright to low mood. But just like any tool, it only works when used in the right time, place and way.

Once, I had a client who was a high-achieving man in his prime. Like many people, he had been taught that exercise is the best form of stress management. As a middle manager at a Fortune 500 company with long working days, he devoted all his free time to marathon running. Telling the manager that his workload was unreasonable wasn't an option – so he would exercise himself happy on his own. Then he found himself in therapy with full-blown burnout. And knee injuries.

Before you use the behaviour principle, I encourage you to STOP. This will help you to figure out what the problem actually is and the best way to manage it. STOP stands for:

- Self-compassion
- Think
- Options
- Practise

This is the process you should go through every time you find yourself slipping into an emotion trap. We will now go through the stages one by one.

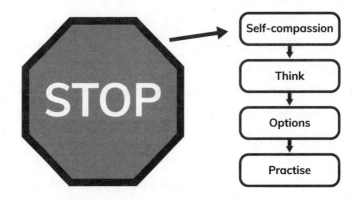

Self-compassion

If you're feeling awful, it's tempting to try to shut down your thoughts and feelings. They can seem like traitors

or enemies that must be fought. But this might be a good time to remind yourself why they are there in the first place. Troubled feelings are a signal that something important to you is at stake, that life isn't the way you want it to be. If, instead of ignoring these feelings, you try to understand them, you can gain invaluable information.

Self-compassion means trying to understand and take care of yourself when you come up against obstacles. Rather than judging or dismissing your emotions, try to show yourself the same empathy as you would show a close friend who found themselves in a similar situation.

You feel the way you do for a reason – often several reasons. You don't have to like, agree with or act on the impulses you have, but taking the time to understand what you feel and why is the first step towards change.

If you try to skip this step, things can go very wrong. Repressing feelings doesn't make them go away; they just manifest in other ways. Jealousy is a common example of this, where people might hide their fear of being rejected behind anger at imagined betrayals. Unfortunately, this rarely leads to the comfort they crave.

If you're not honest about your needs, you won't get them met. So many arguments could be avoided if both parties just stopped and asked themselves: is this really that important to me or am I just upset and tired? Research shows that people who practise self-compassion don't just feel better day to day, they also sleep better, are more resilient in the face of failure and live healthier lives because they take better care of themselves. Self-compassion can help protect you from depression, eating disorders and stress.

So, step one is to stop and tune into your feelings. Put words to what you are thinking and feeling and what your impulses are telling you. Remember that everybody feels jealousy, fear and despair, even if they don't tend to talk about it at a cocktail party. The fact that you feel this way is neither dangerous nor strange.

Complete this sentence: 'It's no wonder that I would feel this way because . . .' List as many reasons as you can come up with.

What would you say to a friend in the same situation? Try saying the same things to yourself. If your friend came up with objections, what would you reply?

It can be difficult to have compassion for yourself, especially in trying situations. But, just as with all things, it gets easier with practice.

Think

If your job is making unreasonable demands then becoming more stress-resistant is not the solution – it's changing your job. If you tend to lose your temper when the kids fight before dinner, family therapy is not the solution – it's a little pre-dinner snack.

The behaviour principle is not a universal solution to all your problems. It doesn't work against colds, bad working environments or hangry family members. It should only be used on emotion traps – i.e. when the problem is that your feelings are somehow 'out of sync' with the rest of your life. They may be disproportionate, misdirected or in conflict with your long-term goals, meaning that acting on them creates problems.

Let's take a few common examples. Maybe you get nervous about something that you logically understand isn't dangerous. And instead of using the behaviour principle and training yourself to reduce your nerves, you fall into an emotion trap. Or maybe you don't feel like seeing people because you feel down. But if socialising usually cheers you up, going out is probably a better idea than staying at home and moping.

However, the behaviour principle should not be used when your reaction is entirely reasonable. Sometimes the smartest thing you can do is follow your emotional impulses – for example, by screaming and running away from genuine danger.

The behaviour principle also doesn't work if your thoughts and feelings are rooted in an undeniable problem. It doesn't matter how much you try to adapt if the conditions for change are impossible. The behaviour principle can help you set a romantic mood but it cannot revive a dead relationship. It can help you maximise joy in your everyday life but it cannot prevent low blood sugar.

So, the next step, after you have shown self-compassion, is to get your thinking cap on. What is really the problem here and what is the best solution? Do you need to adapt or is it your environment that needs to change? If there are real issues behind your thoughts and feelings then deal with them. And if it's just an emotion trap? Continue!

Options

Once you've decided to use the behaviour principle, you need to examine the situation and consider your options. There's no guarantee that your first idea is the best.

If, like many people, you're stuck in the 'couch potato' emotion trap, perhaps your first thought is to sign up for an annual pass at the local gym. That should give you the incentive to exercise! Unfortunately, this can often turn out to be nothing but an expensive mistake. If you don't enjoy the gym, you'll probably have more success with evening walks or meeting your tennis-fanatic friend for a match. This book will give you lots of tips and suggestions for new behaviours. Think of it as a buffet from which you can pick and mix your favourites.

- **What works for you?** Choose behaviours that are appealing and fit in with your habits and interests. This increases your chances of success.

- **Set the bar at the right height.** If the gap between your thoughts, feelings and behaviours is too wide, you'll never be able to keep up your desired changes. It's better to start where you are and raise the bar step by step rather than aim too high and give up. Then again, don't set the bar ridiculously low or it won't have any effect. Behaviour only just outside your comfort zone is usually best.

- **Watch out for subtle behaviours.** You'll never have fun at a party if you stand huddled in a corner all evening. In order for the behaviour principle to work, you need to be open and really devote yourself to your new activity. Pay attention to the little behaviours that fuel the emotion trap.

- **One thing at a time.** Resist the temptation to try to manage your whole life at once. I know it's tempting, especially when you start trying it out and realise it works. Begin with one emotion trap, preferably the one that creates the most problems for you at the moment. Once you've mastered that one, you'll have more time and energy to tackle the next one.

Practise!

There are no perfect solutions. It's good to think and consider different options, but don't get stuck in analysis-paralysis and spend too much time weighing up the pros and cons. Choose the most appealing (or least unappealing) option and put theory into practice. If it doesn't work, you can always go back and try something else.

Preferably, repeat the new behaviour three times before evaluating the effect. Sometimes you get life-changing results straight away, but it can also take a while. The first time you do something, you won't be used to it and might overthink it (*Is this working? How do I look?* and so on). The second time, you'll start to get the hang of it. After the third time, you'll be able to see a pattern and draw conclusions about whether it is worth continuing.

For major behavioural changes, such as changing careers, moving house or getting a pet, I recommend 'cheap tests'. Instead of diving in head first, start with smaller behaviours that can give you a feel for whether the change will suit you or not. For example, if you're curious about changing profession, have lunch with someone who can tell you what it's like from the inside, take a course or apply for a freelance assignment – things that require less time, energy and money than a complete life change.

Speak to Someone

Humans are pack animals and we're not meant to handle everything by ourselves. Although this book focuses on how you can deal with challenges on your own, I strongly recommend that you involve another person, such as a friend, family member or classmate. Self-compassion is good but it can't replace the benefits of being seen and understood by someone else.

Maybe you're afraid of being laughed at. This is often an exaggerated concern but it's true that not everyone is a good listener. It's a skill that requires practice and not everyone has practised. You can start by opening up a little and see how it lands. If it feels okay, you can open up a little more. You can also call a helpline – they are staffed by people who are trained to listen.

Maybe you're a stoic who thinks you don't want to burden others with your problems, that they've got their own worries. But let me ask you this: what would you think if the roles were reversed? If your friend/relative/fellow human was wrestling with troublesome thoughts? Wouldn't you like to know, wouldn't you like to be able to help?

It is through displays of mutual trust, when you take turns being there for each other, that relationships are deepened. By being honest about how you feel, you open yourself up for others to do the same.

If you don't let it show when you're having a hard time, neither will others. Think of it as doing everyone a favour.

You can make it easier for others to support you by being honest about what you need. Is it advice to solve a specific problem or just a sympathetic ear? The first impulse people have when someone is struggling is often to try to solve the situation, including showering that person with good advice, whereas sometimes you just want a hug and a piece of cake. Say what you want and there is more chance that you will get it.

Supporting a Friend

Friends and family are often important pieces of the puzzle in our emotion traps. If someone in your family has arachnophobia then it's likely that other family members have to come to the rescue in times of need and respond at the first scream.

The people around us can exacerbate our emotion traps without knowing it. It's something people often do out of a desire to be kind because they notice that it helps in the moment. You let your friend ruminate – maybe even encourage it – when it might actually make them feel better to think about something else. You encourage your child to avoid things they find difficult instead of supporting them to be brave. It can be hard to know the best way to support someone. If you have a friend who is feeling down should you comfort them, cheer them up or leave them alone?

Once I was a guest on a morning television show and was asked: 'How do you support someone suffering from mental health problems?' I was puzzled – as puzzled as I imagine a doctor would be if someone asked, 'How do you support someone suffering from physical health problems?' The short answer is: the same way you would support anyone going through a difficult time. Let them know you're there for them, listen if they want to talk and offer to make them soup. Beyond that, of course, it depends on what problems the person is facing. People with high blood pressure need an exercise buddy, whereas people who have recently undergone surgery need to be kept company while they lie in bed.

The same is true for the emotion trap. Just being there and showing that you care will go a long way. The best way to support them further depends on what feelings are involved. A stressed person needs help to stop and rest; a depressed person needs help to get up and go. For this reason, each chapter of the book will also include a section on how best to support someone struggling with this specific emotion trap.

Let's Do This!

By this point, I hope you've got a good idea of what the emotion trap is and how you can use the behaviour principle to manage it – in theory.

But you didn't come here for theory, you came for practice. Therefore, the rest of this book is a guide to the most common challenges people battle with: self-esteem, happiness, motivation, anxiety and stress. You will delve deeper into these common emotion traps and learn how to use the behaviour principle to manage them.

I recommend that you read this book from cover to cover – even if a particular area doesn't feel relevant to you right now, it will help you to understand the nuances of the behaviour principle so that you can apply it to other feelings and areas that aren't covered in this book. Feel free to pause and further investigate a specific topic that you want to work on in your everyday life.

Before you use the behaviour principle, remember to STOP. This will make your journey of personal development so much easier, more enjoyable and effective.

CHAPTER 1

The Self-Esteem Myth

The Emotion Trap:
superficial, short-term validation
The Behaviour Principle:
meaningful, long-term validation

In recent decades, the importance of self-esteem has been emphasised time and time again. Perhaps as the most important thing of all. We are taught that people blessed with high self-esteem can stand up for themselves and face life's challenges with strength and courage. They can lounge on the sofa eating junk food all day and then look at themselves in the mirror with an approving smile and think, I'm great.

For us mere mortals, however, self-love is conditional. We stand tall when we receive praise but one critical comment can be enough to ruin an entire evening. There are times when we love ourselves and times when we feel worthless. I've tried every trick in the book to boost my self-esteem. I have spent weeks with my nose in various self-help books and obediently stood in front of the mirror chanting 'you are worthy just as you are'. But guess what? Most of what we've been taught about self-esteem is wrong.

On Self-Esteem

Self-esteem is defined by the value you assign yourself. Whether you deem yourself good enough as you are, here and now, and deserving of respect and appreciation from others.

People with high self-esteem believe that they are at least as valuable as others and generally feel satisfied with themselves, their strengths and weaknesses. People with low self-esteem, on the other hand, can feel like worthless failures. They may underestimate their strengths, exaggerate their shortcomings and have trouble respecting themselves. Hence, these people accept that other people may not respect them either.

When we talk about self-esteem, we are usually referring to what psychology calls global self-esteem – i.e. how you feel about yourself in general. In reality, self-esteem is often divided into subcategories corresponding to different aspects of life. You could picture this as a cake cut into slices, each of which represents a facet of your identity that is important to you. Some of the most common slices are: career, family and appearance. You might also have slices more unique to you, such as ice hockey skills or environmentalism. Depending on how things are going in a particular important area of life – for example, parenthood – you will feel more or less worthy in that domain. Your feelings about each portion of cake add up to your impression of the cake as a whole.

The make-up of a person's cake might change throughout their life. A student who is doing badly at school, for example, might reject the 'academic achievement' slice of their cake and develop an alternative slice labelled 'class rebel'. Hence the student's grades will have less effect on their self-esteem and they might try to gain respect from their peers through bullying and smoking behind the bike sheds instead.

Lately, there has been much talk about performance-based self-esteem. This refers to people who rely on achievements, such as excelling at work, to feel valuable. By definition, we all have performance-based self-esteem. Everyone feels crappy when they perceive themselves to be failing in an important area of life. But not all self-esteem depends on what we would usually define as 'performance', such as professional or academic achievement. Some may value themselves according to more unquantifiable areas of life, such as a partner's love or God's blessing.

Some people say that self-esteem (believing that you have intrinsic worth) is completely different from self-confidence (trusting your ability to handle things).

It is true that self-esteem and self-confidence are two different things but they are often connected. If you tend to succeed in what you set out to do, your self-confidence will grow. If this success is within an area that is important to your sense of identity, your self-esteem will grow along with it.

It is possible to have high self-esteem in one area, such as career, but still have low global self-esteem. Perhaps you are dissatisfied with other important pieces of the cake, such as your love life or appearance.

Self-esteem is not a constant; it fluctuates throughout your life.

It is common for people with perfectionist tendencies to have self-esteem issues. **Perfectionism** means putting excessive effort into trying to make things perfect. If things don't turn out exactly right according to the sky-high standard you have set yourself (zealously cheered on by unattainable social ideals) the result feels worthless.

It's difficult to be the perfect friend, colleague and parent all at the same time. You will learn more about how to overcome perfectionism in the chapter on anxiety.

What is 'normal' self-esteem?

People often talk about self-esteem being high or low, as if they are two distinct categories. In reality, self-esteem is on a sliding scale and most of us fall somewhere in the middle. This applies not only to self-esteem but to most psychological traits – most people are neither absolute introverts nor extroverts but somewhere in between.

Occasional feelings of worthlessness are entirely normal. It is a very unpleasant but not unusual feeling. If you never feel badly about yourself, you have unusually high self-esteem. If you feel useless all the time then your self-esteem is unusually low – and it might be worth considering therapy to do something about it.

The most common test to measure self-esteem in the world of psychology is called the Rosenberg Self-Esteem Scale. You will find it at the back of this book. The questionnaire can assess whether your self-esteem is high, low, or somewhere in between, as compared to most people.

Self-esteem is not a constant; it fluctuates throughout your life. There is a widespread misconception that self-esteem largely depends on how we were treated by our parents in childhood, whether they were loving or dismissive. In fact, up to 40 per cent of your self-esteem tendencies are determined by genes. Just as we are born with different genetic predispositions in terms of height and shoe size, we are born with different temperaments. Some people are more confident in themselves by nature.

About 15–30 per cent of self-esteem is fluid and changes throughout life. Most people suffer from lower self-esteem as children and teens. It usually gets a boost in young adulthood when people start to understand their identities, what they want out of life and how to get it. Then self-esteem tends to increase steadily and peaks somewhere around the age of 60–70. By this time, most people have found contexts in which they feel needed and appreciated.

Setbacks can cause self-esteem to plummet. Illness, unemployment and divorce often create gaps in the self-esteem cake that can only heal when the lost slice is replaced with something else.

Self-esteem often takes a hit when you become a parent. Especially for women, studies show. It is difficult to 'succeed' as a parent by modern standards. Putting food on the table and providing loving arms to crawl to aren't always considered enough. Some people feel

WHAT IS NORMAL SELF-ESTEEM?

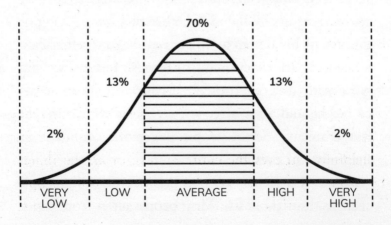

like a terrible parent if they don't cook everything from scratch using local, organic ingredients.

The Emotion Trap

So, your self-esteem depends on how various important aspects of your life are going at any given time. The idea of anyone being totally independent and not caring about what other people think is utter rubbish. Most of us depend on validation and achievement to feel good about ourselves, but how we go about getting that validation can differ. And this 'how' can be the difference between success and disaster.

There are various things that can bring about a decline in self-esteem. Maybe your confidence has been knocked – for example, by being fired or heartbroken. Or perhaps your self-worth was standing on shaky ground to begin with and a gentle nudge was all it took to push you over the edge. One strange look, one bad review, one changing room with unflattering lighting and bang! You start spiralling round the psychological triangle. Your thoughts turn dark. You become your own biggest critic. You call yourself an idiot, a loser or whatever insults feed your self-hatred. Maybe old mistakes come back to haunt you. Your brain helpfully retrieves the entire archive of all the things you've ever done wrong. You think about other people who you perceive as having their lives together and it really hammers home how much of a failure you are compared to them. If anyone tries to cheer you up and reassure you that you're a good person with many great qualities, it sounds like lies. You can't see any of your strengths, only your flaws. Anything you've ever accomplished was just down to dumb luck and coincidence, you decide.

Of course, none of this is true, but it can seem this way temporarily when a negative emotional filter settles over your thoughts. This is because your feelings are also affected by your setback. You feel depressed and deflated. Maybe you are ashamed and feel unworthy of love. Even if you get another opportunity for a date or job interview, or whatever, you have no desire to take it. What's the point?

When your thoughts and feelings are this dark, it affects your behaviour. Your impulses tell you to forget everything and give up. Then, because you need validation (as we all do), hopelessness is often followed by an intense desire for vindication. You work extra hard to prove that the person who criticised you is wrong or you desperately seek validation elsewhere.

These are normal reactions. No one is immune to setbacks and we all have days when our self-esteem takes a beating. But, depending on your general foundation of self-esteem, and how you have learned to cope with these low points, you might get stuck in a negative loop in the psychological triangle.

Do you recognise any of these common emotion traps?

- **Over-performing.** You set out to prove that you are in fact worthy. You push yourself to make everything perfect and surpass expectations. No one must have any reason to criticise you whatsoever!

- **People pleasing.** You become a yes-sayer, terrified of rejection if you cause anyone the slightest inconvenience. You do things for everyone except yourself.

- **Attention seeking.** If the validation you need doesn't come spontaneously, you make sure to seek it out. You become boastful and proud, making yourself the centre of attention at the expense of others. If anyone criticises you, you immediately dismiss them as an idiot or a hater.

- **Quick fixes.** Expensive designer clothes, scantily clad selfies, extramarital flirtations . . . There are a thousand ways to get a quick self-esteem boost. Of course, there's nothing wrong with relishing the occasional compliment from strangers in the pub, but as a strategy to boost fragile self-esteem, it quickly becomes destructive.

The price? As with all emotion traps, you result in shooting yourself in the foot. Even if your self-esteem gets a temporary lift the effect is short-lived. The hunt just begins again the next day. You ask yourself what's wrong, why aren't you being appreciated for who you really are? What if you really are worthless? You don't feel seen or genuinely appreciated.

The worst case scenario is getting stuck in a negative spiral. Low self-esteem can exacerbate existing problems with anxiety, depression and eating disorders. You get tangled up in guilt, lies and conflicts – all for the sake of winning a few crumbs of validation.

Are You an Imposter?

It's easy to imagine that everyone except you is going around feeling great about themselves all the time. This is because people rarely advertise their own weaknesses.

Studies have shown that one in ten people suffer from what is known as **imposter syndrome**, which is a pop-psychology term for going through life feeling like a fake who might be exposed at any moment. Everyone else comes across as comfortable and competent, while you hide behind a facade. As many as eight in ten people report feeling like an imposter from time to time.

The best way to prick a hole in imposter syndrome is to talk about it. If you bring it up with colleagues at the pub after work, you are bound to find that someone else is relieved to discover that they are not the only 'imposter' at the office.

There is a whole industry of quick fixes for people struggling with low self-esteem. You're encouraged to write compliments on Post-it notes or tell your reflection in the mirror that you are a good person. You can listen to inspirational speakers or download pep talks full of positive affirmations.

I tend to see these exercises as icing on the self-esteem cake. Icing is nice, it looks pretty and some might seep into the cake underneath, if you're lucky. But decorating the cake isn't enough to achieve meaningful results. You have to delve in and work on the slices themselves.

The Behaviour Principle

Instead of waiting for the confidence to speak up, speak up now – even though it's uncomfortable. Instead of dreaming of one day having time for self-care, switch off your phone and run yourself a bath right now. Instead of staying up until 2am scouring your report for typos, add a typo in on purpose and go to bed.

It feels very unnatural. You're probably dubious that it will work. But this is how to change the direction of movement around the psychological triangle and give your self-esteem room to grow.

It's perfectly logical if you think about it. It's hard

to respect yourself if you let others walk all over you. Hard to know what you long for if you're always suppressing your own needs for the sake of others'. Hard to build genuine relationships if you are busy with superficial pastimes.

The psychological triangle forewarns that it will probably feel unpleasant at first before your thoughts and feelings have caught up with your actions. You feel guilty, cocky. Your mind is filled with doubt. Don't worry. Persevere and you will find that your self-esteem catches on eventually.

What would higher self-esteem entail for you? For some, it might be the humility to apologise; for others, it could be the confidence to stand up for themselves. To find out what self-esteem means to you, try finishing these sentences:

- I can tell when someone has high self-esteem because . . .
- If I had higher self-esteem I would . . .
- Others would notice that I had higher self-esteem if I stopped . . . and started . . .

This chapter is about giving your self-esteem room to grow. We will look at how to resist the shortcuts to superficial validation and invest in large-scale infrastructure instead.

Five Myths about Self-Esteem

Myth 1: Your self-esteem is defined by your childhood.

Reality: Your self-esteem is about 40 per cent genetic and 15–30 per cent how your life is going, here and now.

Myth 2: You have a general level of self-esteem that pertains to every aspect of your life.

Reality: Self-esteem varies between different facets of your life. You can have, say, high self-esteem in your career but low self-esteem when it comes to your appearance.

Myth 3: There is no correlation between self-esteem and self-confidence.

Reality: Self-esteem (feeling valuable) and self-confidence (feeling capable or competent) are two different things but are often connected. Your self-esteem is boosted when you succeed in areas that are important to you.

Myth 4: People with high self-esteem are more successful and popular.

Reality: High self-esteem has been proven to be an advantage in specific situations. For example, having the courage to get up and try again after a setback. But overall, self-esteem doesn't play all that big a role in your success. Nor in relationships. There are plenty of successful, popular people with low self-esteem – and plenty of fools convinced of their own brilliance.

However, self-esteem significantly influences how you feel. And that's as good a reason as any to work on yours!

Myth 5: The best way to boost your self-esteem is to say positive things to yourself.

Reality: The best way to boost your self-esteem is to make progress within important areas of your life and to stick to contexts where you feel needed and appreciated.

What to Do

Bake your own self-esteem cake

Now I want you to get out a pencil and paper (or fire up Excel, if that's what you're into). Draw a circle and divide it into several pieces to represent your self-esteem cake. Make them different sizes depending on how important they are to your self-esteem. Some common slices tend to be family, career, love, friendship and appearance, but yours may vary.

It might help to think about questions such as: 'If I had a real setback in this area of life, how bad would I feel?' or 'If I did really well in this area, how pleased would I be with myself as a person?'

The resulting cake will vary from person to person. Here are a few red flags that indicate it might be time to bake yourself a new self-esteem cake from scratch.

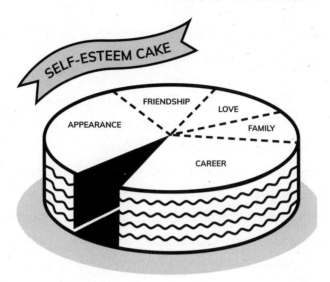

One piece dominates

Some people have a large slice that dominates almost the entire cake – perhaps 'career' or 'relationships'. If a large proportion of your self-esteem is dependent on a single aspect, you are likely to face dramatic ups and downs in your self-esteem depending on how things are going in that area of your life. You might be on top of the world when things are going well at work or you receive validation from your partner, and then feel completely worthless if you don't get your next validation fix.

Then, if you get stuck in the emotion trap this can become a negative spiral, where one piece of cake grows at the expense of the others. You become so concerned with succeeding in this important area that you push everything else aside until you wake up and realise your entire sense of self-worth is in the hands of your boss. This would mean you need to invest more in other areas of life. If you look closely, you will find other important pieces, such as 'friends' and 'hobbies'. Put more time and energy into them and they will grow over time.

A missing piece

If you suffer a loss, your self-esteem often takes a beating. Especially if it happens suddenly. This might be a break-up, losing your job or an injury that restricts your activity.

It's all too easy to feel worthless when something that once gave your life meaning suddenly disappears. Trust me: it does get better. Time passes and other things grow to fill the void. You can help this process along by consciously setting out to invest in other meaningful aspects of your life, such as deepening important relationships.

Some people also manage to redefine what it means to 'succeed' in a certain area. Perhaps winning medals is no longer essential to your identity as a sportsperson and you can feel the same sense of accomplishment by nurturing the next generation of talent.

An unhealthy piece

Maybe you discover pieces of cake that you would rather weren't there, that you don't feel good about. For people suffering from eating disorders, 'weight' may be a bigger factor than 'career' and 'family' combined. Maybe you derive your self-worth from crime, adultery or destructive online forums.

Finding these parts of yourself and accepting that they are problematic is a difficult process. After all, they are a source of validation that you can't or don't want to live without. Unfortunately, they have to be dealt with in order for you to live a happy life. It doesn't matter how much icing you spread on a mouldy slice of cake. You need to get to the root of the problem – for example, by going to therapy.

Think about how you spend your time on a typical day. Are the most important pieces of the cake getting the time and love they deserve? Are there pieces that are getting too much of your energy? You can adjust the size of your slices by re-prioritising. It can be difficult to resist, of course, because your thoughts and feelings argue that it is time well spent. Don't be fooled.

How would you rather spend your time? The best way to stop one behaviour is to start another.

Do things that make you feel good about yourself

In Western culture, we like the idea that we can feel good about ourselves apropos of nothing. The dream is to be able to lie in a hammock thinking: *Here I am and I'm good enough*. Not only is this state difficult to achieve, there is the question of whether this is even an honourable ideal to pursue. It says a lot about our modern individualistic culture that we try to improve our self-esteem by standing in front of the mirror and telling ourselves that we're good enough rather than seeking out activities and contexts where others tell us so.

Resilient self-esteem is built by making progress in important areas of your life. This includes good deeds that make you feel proud of yourself.

Is 'friendships' one of your pieces of cake? Celebrate your friends' successes and listen attentively when they talk about their day. Do you have a piece called 'appearance'? Give away the clothes you keep in the back of your closet for when you 'reach your target weight' and buy clothes that make you feel good about yourself right now.

We do not have to win industry awards or look like a model to feel good about ourselves. What counts here isn't any particular achievement but the feeling that you are developing in the right direction. For many of my clients suffering from depression, just starting to wash their hair regularly is a big step. So that's where we begin.

I once spent a summer working as a care assistant in a nursing home. The facility housed a wonderful variety of people, from the retired footballer who never stopped talking about his match-winning goal in the summer of 1947 to the glamourpuss who always wore a tie-neck blouse and kept a cheese platter in the fridge.

However, many of the residents felt that they had come to the end of the line. Without everyday duties and commitments, all that remained was to pass the time and wait for death. There was nothing to boost their self-esteem. So we set about finding ways to add meaning in their lives. Climbing mountains and starting businesses was off the cards for practical reasons, but we could write postcards to relatives and organise tea parties. I taught an elderly gentleman how to fold napkins and he went on to delight the other residents with small works of art awaiting them on their dinner plates. We made an effort to look dapper for Friday night dinner, getting dressed up for the occasion.

What makes you feel proud? Based on your current circumstances, here and now?

You might also want to think about whether there is something gnawing at your conscience. Such things can do a lot to harm your self-esteem. Owning up to and apologising for your mistakes can be painful at the time, but you will probably feel better in the long run if you take responsibility for your actions. The same applies to becoming a vegan, donating to charity or making more environmentally conscious decisions, if these are things that weigh on your conscience. It's hard to feel good about yourself if you're not following your own ethical compass.

Of course, you can't do everything. You can't be the perfect parent, friend, co-worker and partner while also dedicating time to your own wellbeing. You have to prioritise. So the question is – what's most important to you? Of all the things you could do today, what would make you most proud of yourself when you stand in front of the mirror tonight and look yourself in the eye? What about when you look back on this time in five, fifteen or fifty years? This is the priority for your self-esteem.

THE SELF-ESTEEM MOVEMENT

In the United States, the self-esteem hype peaked in the 1980s. Studies showed that people with high self-esteem experienced better health, relationships and academic performance than those with lower self-esteem. Feel-good gurus started encouraging positive affirmations with your breakfast cereal. Special school programmes were even introduced to boost students' self-esteem.

The movement came to an abrupt halt in 2003. This was when an extensive compilation of scientific research was released showing that while the self-esteem of the American population had indeed increased, public health and school results hadn't improved. If anything, they had got worse.

People with high self-esteem may have perceived themselves as more popular or intelligent than others but it wasn't necessarily true. It seemed that success boosted self-esteem rather than the other way around. And it was argued that school students who had been taught unconditional self-love risked becoming more narcissistic than their peers.

Psychologists no longer advocate interventions that primarily target self-esteem. Now they recommend encouraging personal development and good deeds, which are more likely to make us feel valued and welcome, regardless of where we end up in life. Nevertheless, the old beliefs live on. It would be fair to question why we are drawn to self-love exercises like cats to catnip. Could it be because the idea that there is one universal reason behind self-hatred and anxiety, which we can easily cure with ten minutes of daily positive affirmations, is a very convenient one? Maybe because self-love exercises feel good in the moment and reap short-term results.

The behaviour principle is more like a sweaty workout: difficult at the time but brings about positive results in the long run.

Nurture your relationships

People often talk about the need for validation as if it's a bad thing. In reality, we all need it – humans are herd animals, after all. The real question is how we get it.

If you have low self-esteem, it is tempting to seek superficial validation. There is nothing necessarily wrong with fishing for compliments or likes, but the effect is often short-lived. Longer-term validation tends to come from close relationships. People who like you for who you are, who value and need you. People who support you through tough times and don't judge you when you screw up. So one of the best things you can do for your self-esteem is invest in your relationships. Find people you want in your life, and who want you in theirs, and then savour the relationship like a gourmet chocolate truffle. Spend time with those people, support them and try to overcome setbacks together.

Romantic relationships are one of the most important sources of self-esteem for many adults. There is something very reassuring about feeling loved even when you are sitting on the sofa in your PJs. You can also get validation from relatives, friends, pets or close colleagues. People who know you inside and out, and still light up when you enter a room.

Self-esteem is also fortified when you feel part of a larger community context. This could be a club, a circle of friends or a congregation where you have a place and feel valued. If you have such a context it is usually worth holding on to. If not, consider finding one.

Do you have an interest that you want to share with others? An issue you are committed to? Volunteering is often dynamite for self-esteem because you get to contribute to something you believe in, gain appreciation from those around you and become part of a larger community.

Unfortunately, the opposite is also true. Bad relationships can undermine self-esteem. It's difficult to feel good about yourself if you are regularly being insulted or dismissed. It's challenging, if not impossible, to cultivate higher self-esteem when you have a partner, boss or relative who criticises everything you do.

The first step is to draw attention to the issue. Many social bulldozers aren't aware of what they are doing when they ride roughshod over others' self-esteem and the effect it has. They need someone to speak up, kindly but firmly. Remember that the self-esteem of bulldozers can also be sensitive to criticism. If you bring it up politely, you will have a better chance of the other person taking your points on board rather than immediately going on the defensive.

If you have raised the matter several times and nothing has changed, it may be time to ask yourself whether this is really a relationship you want to keep. Sometimes you need to minimise contact with someone in order to protect your health. On occasion, the only option is to end a relationship.

This can bring up a lot of sadness. You might think back to your upbringing and all the times you were treated unfairly. Children need love and encouragement to grow, yet many have faced rejection and abuse. If this is the case you should know that it is never too late. The past has shaped the person you are today but the present is what matters most. Putting the past behind you and focusing on the contexts in which you feel empowered and appreciated can heal old wounds. It won't remove the scars but it can help you feel whole and give you hope for the future.

Just be careful not to get too obsessed with your own personal development. The pursuit of self-esteem can, paradoxically, do more harm than good if you become so absorbed in your own feelings that you forget about the people around you. People with high self-esteem rarely spend time evaluating and analysing themselves. They are too busy with their relationships and commitments.

THE ALGORITHM BEHIND OBSESSION

Sometimes people become trapped in relationships that are downright destructive. Your relationship might be characterised by frequent arguments and betrayal – perhaps even violence – and yet you are drawn to the other person like a moth to a flame.

'Why don't you just break up?' sigh your exasperated friends, and you may ask yourself the same question.

The answer is: intermittent reinforcement.

Intermittent reinforcement is psychology speak for a random schedule of rewards. When you embark on a relationship, it tends to be because of the benefits of being around the other person: excitement, intimacy, an excuse to ignore the laundry. If the good feelings are intense enough, the occasional argument doesn't matter. You always find your way back to intimacy afterwards. You get your emotional fix.

The arguments may become more frequent. But if in between you are 'rewarded' for your patience with romantic promises and expressions of love, you stick it out. You live in hope that one day you will be able to find your way back to paradise.

If I asked you whether you would like to date someone who, in a year from now, will ignore your messages and leave you crying in a heap on the floor, I'm pretty sure your answer would be no. It is the gradual decline that makes it so treacherous. As the relationship takes up more and more space in your life, you become dependent on your partner's validation. Eventually, your entire self-esteem cake is governed by your relationship and it feels like you would be nothing without it.

It's not your fault – this is how people work when a sufficiently tempting reward is dangled just out of reach. Intermittent reinforcement explains why people get stuck in all sorts of unhealthy behaviours, from gambling addiction (what if I'm about to hit the jackpot?) and endless social media scrolling (what if I'm about to stumble on something amazing?) to ruminating on the past (what if I could finally understand?). If you expect the much-coveted reward to be out there somewhere, you will continue tirelessly.

There is a way out. Alas, it can be difficult to accept. You need to replace the unhealthy piece of cake with something else entirely. Build on other relationships and find new pastimes that give you what you need. If you find it difficult to succeed on your own help is out there – you are not alone.

Say thank you for compliments

How do you talk about yourself in front of other people? Joking about your own shortcomings can make you feel safe because you're getting in there before anyone else gets a chance. Loud self-criticism can also be an unconscious way of fishing for compliments because the people around you will often object and state emphatically that of course you're good-looking/smart/talented.

However, talking yourself down can erode self-esteem in the same way that criticism from other people does. Some humility is healthy but you will never hear someone with high self-esteem call themselves a worthless idiot.

Think about how you talk about yourself. When you get home in the evening and recount your day, don't just list all the ways you've messed up. Mention the things you are proud of as well. You don't need to brag but try to give a balanced picture. This also applies when you receive compliments. Don't immediately dismiss them with an 'Oh, I wasn't really happy with it.' Practise saying, 'Thank you, I'm glad you like it.'

You might also want to consider how you talk to yourself in your own mind. Are you critical, neutral or friendly in tone? The next time you make a mistake, try writing down your inner monologue word for word. If you're unlucky, it might go something like this: 'How could I have made such an embarrassing joke? I really am the worst. No wonder no one wants to spend time with me.'

How would you respond to a friend who said this about themselves? Write down your response and try saying it to yourself. The idea isn't to turn criticism into unconditional praise but to be a little more understanding. 'Nobody laughed at the joke, but at least I tried. Maybe I need to find people who share my sense of humour.'

Your actions have an effect here and it's easy to get stuck in habits that feed self-criticism. Maybe you follow influencers who reinforce your complexes or you spend hours examining yourself critically in the mirror. Free yourself from all these unnecessary triggers. Unfollow social media accounts that make you feel bad about yourself. Find positive, feel-good fitness inspiration or simply delete that app. If you need to use a mirror, do what you must and then stop looking. Don't start picking at moles, poking at wrinkles or squeezing folds of skin. Avoid any discussion of diets, brands or exercise regimes that feed your complexes.

I haven't opened a women's magazine since the age of 18 when I panicked over an article with the head-line: 'What your choice of dinner says about your relationship.' According to that magazine, not only was I failing in my skincare routine, negotiation techniques and choice of mascara, but my penchant for pasta would be the death of my relationship.

I cancelled my subscription.

Stand up for your needs

When you struggle with low self-esteem, it can be difficult to strike the right balance between your own needs and the needs of others. You might be a validation addict, constantly seeking approval but very sensitive to criticism. If anybody challenges you it feeds your innermost fear: that you are worthless and unlovable.

At its core, the problem is the same, but there are two very different strategies for dealing with this need for validation. I call them the Doormat and the Balloon. This is a crude generalisation but I think you will recognise the types.

The Doormat lays low and never causes problems. They try to please and don't contradict others unnecessarily. By never taking a stand, they hope to avoid any form of criticism. But it's impossible to keep everybody happy. 'Why do you always have to be so nice?' the Doormat often hears.

The Balloon is the exact opposite of the Doormat. The Balloon inflates themselves and takes up space at the expense of others. They never admit to a fault and brag about their exploits. At first glance, it may seem that the Balloon has very high self-esteem, or at least a lot of self-confidence. But in reality, inflated egos are often fragile and punctured by the slightest poke.

The happy medium between these two strategies is **assertiveness**. This means that you take your own needs and the needs of others equally seriously. You stand up for your opinion but respect that others may think differently. You admit your mistakes without beating yourself up too much.

Assertiveness can be developed using the behaviour principle. Exactly which behaviours you need to practise depends on whether you lean more towards being a Doormat or a Balloon – or a mix of both. Here are a few ideas.

Exercises for Doormats

'If I had higher self-esteem I would stand up for myself.' Forget that! We're changing direction around the psychological triangle. It is by taking up space that your self-esteem will have room to grow.

- State your thoughts and preferences in a variety of situations. Bring up an opposing opinion in a discussion and stand up for it. Speak up in meetings and talk for the same length of time as the others do.

- Come up with suggestions. Sometimes they flop, as happens to everyone when proposing a film or restaurant. Do it anyway.

- Apologise when you have done something wrong. But never if you haven't.

- Express your needs. When you are clear about what you need, you are giving other people the opportunity to take it into account.

- Make your own decisions. Practise not asking for advice unless you need it.

- If someone does something that you're not okay with, say so. Be polite but clear. It can be difficult but try to get used to the idea that we are all the villain in someone else's story.

- Stop committing to things that you don't want to do or don't have time for. Stop offering lifts, fitting into other people's schedules and putting duty above all else. Practise rejecting responsibility for other people's problems.

Exercises for Balloons

Inflating yourself and eschewing criticism can work to protect your pride in the short term. Unfortunately, it tends to push people away in the long run. Practise being generous.

- Say, 'You're right.' It can feel unbearable (I know this from personal experience) but I promise it gets easier over time.

- Allow other people time to talk. Listen and ask follow-up questions to resist the temptation to try to think of a story to trump theirs.

- Apologise for messing up or being late. No excuses, just an apology.

- Look for compromises. Let others have their way and try to adapt to their needs.

- When other people do things without you, try not to take it personally. Wish them all the best and dedicate the time to doing something you enjoy.

- Let other people win arguments when they make better points than you. Your worth as a person doesn't depend on winning – be magnanimous.

This isn't going to be easy. When trying these out for the first time it can be like downing a cocktail of shame, anxiety and discomfort. Your self-esteem may feel more fragile than ever. Stick it out! Remember that the behaviour principle requires several repetitions before you see results. It's just like training a muscle. Start practising in easier situations and soon you will feel more comfortable to move on to bigger challenges.

You might come up against resistance. You might say the wrong thing, get a no or be misunderstood. It happens to everyone. If everyone gave up at these hurdles then no one would ever reach a point where they were able to get married or be promoted. Think of it as a temporary extra weight on your dumbbell – if you push through, you'll come out the other side stronger than ever.

Supporting a Friend

As we have seen, validation from the people around you is not necessarily the most important thing for self-esteem, welcome though it may be. The key is to have several contexts in which you feel well-liked and competent.

If you have a friend or family member who chronically doubts themselves, the best support you can give is to encourage them to seek out these contexts. Give your partner time to keep up with band rehearsals or meet up with the old gang. Encourage your friend to take the next step in their career. Enrol your bubbly child in circus school and your shy one onto a writing course so that they can both find contexts in which their idiosyncrasies become their strengths.

When someone we care about is feeling fragile, our first impulse is often to do things for them. This comes from a place of kindness, but feeling capable and useful is also important for self-esteem. Ask them to help you with something that they are good at, whether that's fixing the Wi-Fi router or giving good advice. Show that you appreciate their help.

Of course, you want this person to feel that your relationship is one of the contexts in which they feel liked and appreciated. This doesn't usually need to be stated in words if you are happy to see them and share laughter and tears with them. But saying it out loud can also be a bonus – being told that you mean a lot to someone is a big self-esteem boost.

There is a misconception, especially with children, that praising achievements can be harmful. Instead of saying, 'What a lovely drawing' (praising achievement), you're supposed to say, 'Tell me about it' (showing interest). The logic behind this is to avoid encouraging performance-based self-esteem, whereby someone believes they have to accomplish things in order to be valued by others. This is a myth. Go ahead and praise people's achievements. Self-esteem is boosted when people feel competent in areas of their life that are important to them, as we have seen. Just don't only praise achievements. Tell your partner that they look good when they're dressed up to go out and when they're watching TV in their jammies. This makes them feel valuable for both who they are and what they do.

A note on affirmation: some people with low self-esteem get stuck in a pattern of criticising themselves in front of others precisely because it usually leads to affirmation. When someone complains about how ugly, hopeless or awful they are, friends immediately rush to their defence. Everyone does this sometimes; it's a social norm. But be on the lookout for an emotion trap, where someone's self-criticism becomes increasingly harsh in order to satisfy a growing need for validation. As this problem worsens, you risk becoming a cog in the machine.

This person needs validation but not as a reward for criticising themselves. Shower them in love at other times – when they've said something clever, made you laugh or just been their wonderful self. You could respond to the self-criticism with more general comfort: 'I'm sorry you feel that way. Is there anything I can do to make you feel better?' You could also mention that you don't like hearing anyone speak badly about your friend, even if it's coming from the friend themselves. Maybe you can come to an agreement that self-hatred is banned and work together to find more constructive ways to manage self-doubt.

CHAPTER 2

Schedule in Joy

The Emotion Trap: passivity
The Behaviour Principle: activity

On Happiness

G iven the choice, we would stay in the psychological triangle of happiness all the time.

You wake up on the right side of bed, feeling alert and energetic. Your good mood influences your thoughts and you find yourself daydreaming over your morning coffee, thinking of everything you have to look forward to. You feel empowered and motivated – maybe you'll repaint the cupboard doors?

Your good mood affects your behaviour. You say a cheery hello to the bus driver. A bit of rain can't dampen your spirits if you're feeling this good – you lift your face and enjoy the sensation of raindrops on your skin.

Then there are the bad days. When you're feeling down you can't find pleasure even in the things you usually enjoy. Your coffee tastes bitter, you feel sluggish, restless, you don't know what to do with yourself.

Low mood places a grey filter over your thoughts. You find it difficult to remember the good times or see the point in anything. Instead, your mind is occupied with life's hardships and all the mistakes you have ever made. You interpret ambiguities from those around you as personal criticism and proof of what you have always known deep down – that your life is pointless and existence is meaningless. If the bus driver says hello, you give him a sour look, then wallow in guilt for the rest of the bus ride. You put off answering your messages and let the dirty dishes pile up.

Scientists believe that negative emotions such as melancholy fulfil an important function for human beings. Happiness is easier to understand; you feel open, strong and curious, dare to dream big and embark on projects. Melancholy acts as a brake to ensure you keep your feet on the ground. You become focused on your problems and how to deal with them. When you encounter adversity, you are discouraged and retreat to lick your wounds and conserve your energy in order to fight another day.

Having difficult days or weeks is perfectly normal, perhaps even necessary. But just like other feelings, melancholy can become an emotion trap. Protracted, painful and, in some extreme cases, fatal.

The Emotion Trap

Melancholy encourages withdrawal. When nothing seems appealing, you don't just stop making plans for the future, you might also stop doing the things you usually enjoy. You can't be bothered to exercise or socialise. You're not exactly in the mood to sing karaoke.

Instead, you stay at home and kill time on the computer or in front of the TV, crack open a beer or comfort eat ice cream just for something to do. The lack of activities leaves plenty of time for brooding. Because there is a negative filter on your thoughts, they often circle back to how lonely and pointless everything feels. Maybe you scroll through social media looking enviously at all the happy pictures of your friends singing karaoke.

If this negative spiral continues for long enough, it can lead to clinical depression. **Depression** is defined by unusually low mood for several weeks at a time and no longer finding pleasure in things you used to enjoy. It is one of the most common diseases in our society, affecting one in three women and one in five men at some point in their lives. You probably know someone struggling with depression right now.

Periods of depression are often triggered by upheavals, such as divorce or sickness. Things that used to bring joy and meaning to your life – going out with friends, laughter, responsibilities – have disappeared. Or maybe the decline is subtler. Increasing workload and less time to spend with friends and family can slowly and gradually suck the meaning out of life. Even seemingly positive changes, such as having a baby or starting a new study course, can trigger depression because you lose your old routines and sources of joy.

Often depression will fade on its own as life goes on and things change. But if you get stuck in the emotion trap, it can continue its downhill course. Life becomes unbearable. Nothing appeals. You postpone and cancel plans. You become aggressive and self-hating. Meeting friends or facing your problems feels like too daunting a task and you withdraw more and more. Eventually, you can barely get out of bed; you pull the covers over your head and lie there with dark thoughts as your only company.

If you identify with this description, contact your doctor. The behaviour principle can be used to treat clinical depression but when you're feeling this low, it is difficult to succeed on your own. Depression can also have an underlying biological cause, in which case other methods of treatment are necessary.

If, however, you are experiencing 'normal' low mood, then this chapter is for you.

When you are down, you will probably be showered with well-meaning advice from all directions. 'Think positive' is a classic. Unfortunately, it is difficult to see the upside of a painful custody battle or lacking the energy to do the dishes. When you're blue, the negative filter over your thoughts makes looking on the bright side harder than usual.

Some make an effort to 'choose happiness'. But you probably know by now what I think about trying to change emotions through sheer willpower.

The Behaviour Principle

Now I'm going to reveal the single most revolutionary insight I gained from five years of psychology studies: doing fun things makes you happy.

Before you close this book and retire it to the back of the bookshelf (behind the front row of books where there is nothing but dust bunnies, old receipts and a forgotten screw), hear me out.

Feeling down is a sign that your life is not going the way you would like it to. That you lack context, sources of joy or a higher purpose. Or maybe you have all these things on paper but you have stopped engaging with them. From this perspective, there is nothing 'wrong' with you for having the blues. On the contrary, it is an important emotional signal that something needs to change in your everyday life in order for you to thrive again.

When you are down, it can feel like your depressed mood is the problem. You believe that you have to stop feeling unhappy in order to act differently. In fact, the opposite is true. Changing your habits will change the emotion. The behaviour principle is about pushing back against your feelings of melancholy and disinterest and doing the things that usually fill you with joy and energy. Even if it's not as fun as it usually is. Seek out the community you long for, even if it's difficult at first.

This is how you break free from the iron grip of the emotion trap. You feel just a tiny bit better – better than if you were lying on the sofa and staring at the ceiling, anyway. With more things to look forward to, getting up in the morning becomes a little easier. Your thoughts become more optimistic. Your energy grows and you have more strength to face your problems. Step by step, your lust for life creeps back in. The negative cycle around the psychological triangle has been turned into a positive one.

A friend of mine went through this exact process over the course of six months. After losing his job and being dumped by his girlfriend, his days were spent sifting through job ads and grieving the life he had lost. It was midwinter and he didn't even bother turning on the lights as he sat in solitude, binge-watching *The Office* to keep anxiety at bay. He tried online dating but found it difficult to maintain light-hearted, charming conversation and the women he met soon stopped responding to his messages. He saw friends but mostly stayed on the periphery, absorbed in his own thoughts.

The turnaround came after three months. Well-meaning advice from friends and family finally hit home and he realised he didn't want to go on like this. Eagerly encouraged by those around him, he deleted the dating apps and scheduled specific times for job hunting. When possible, he did so with friends who could keep him accountable and make sure he wasn't cheating with a bit of Netflix. He spent the rest of his time reviving old interests and friendships. Salvation came, unexpectedly, in the form of a saxophone. An old childhood dream of being able to play 'Careless Whisper' inspired saxophone lessons and a couple of months later he proudly (albeit imperfectly) honked out his first ABBA songs.

This isn't a question of pretending to be happy. You don't have to go to parties, plaster on a fake grin or do anything else that feels forced. Neither do you have to put on your workout clothes and hit the running track if life feels so chaotic that even walking to the bus stop is a struggle. It's about finding things that genuinely make you feel good. Things that are meaningful to you. And approach them step by step, even if it's difficult at first. Gradually, your thoughts and feelings will catch on.

Let me explain further.

What to Do

Find your feel-good activities

What makes you feel good? If you're lucky, you will be able to think of lots of answers to this question.

It might occur to you that it's been a while since you last saw your friends or went to a football match.

Or maybe you have trouble coming up with anything. Your life is filled with duty and responsibility. Maybe you have never really stopped and asked yourself what you actually enjoy.

I want you to sit down and write a list of your feel-good activities. Anything from feeding the birds and baking bread to buying a new car or going on holiday to Greece. If you need inspiration, I will provide you with a list of possible examples shortly. If you have a calendar you can go back a few weeks and think about the things you have done recently that have 'sparked joy'.

Do it now. You won't find a better opportunity.

You might want to split the activities up into different categories. It's not like you can drink champagne in a jacuzzi every evening. List things you can do alone and others you can do with your family or partner. Simple things that you can do on an average weeknight and bigger projects that require effort. Things that involve action and others that are more relaxed.

I should emphasise that feel-good activities don't necessarily have to be fun. There are plenty of things that can feel rewarding and meaningful even though they are super hard work, like weight training, cleaning out the garage or volunteering to help vulnerable children. The point is to find things that make you feel good in the long term, though temporary pleasures such as sex and wine are also welcome.

Don't include distractions or emotion traps – things that you easily get caught up in but that don't actually make you feel good. Maybe you spend hours watching YouTube or have found that gambling temporarily relieves feelings of emptiness. If anything, write them down on a separate 'feel-bad' list.

Maybe you're stuck. You try but can't think of anything you want to do. If you have felt this way for several weeks, you should talk to someone because it could be clinical depression. However, if it's just a temporary dip, have a go at writing down anything you think you might possibly enjoy. What have you enjoyed in the past? What do other people seem to enjoy?

Not that I would recommend basing your ideas of fun on other people's. I spent my teenage years in clothes shops and at house parties and couldn't understand why I was so unhappy. It wasn't until adulthood that it dawned on me that there might not be anything wrong with me. I was just spending my time in contexts that didn't suit me.

It is possible to be clinically depressed and productive at the same time. Your calendar is fully booked but not with things that you find particularly enjoyable or meaningful. You schedule in things you feel you 'should' do, rather than what you really long to do.

This exercise can bring about a lot of eureka

moments. A common discovery in therapy is that some people simply don't enjoy spending time alone. When you hang out with friends, you tend to treat yourselves to good food and entertainment, but when you're home alone, you might eat a ready meal and watch TV to pass the hours. Perhaps you need to find more meaningful ways to spend your alone time.

You might also discover that relationships that used to be filled with feel-good activities have become predictable and dreary as the realities of everyday life have overtaken the joys. Can you think of something fun you could do together? If you have a partner, when was the last time you got dressed up and went out on a date?

Things you can do:

Do a jigsaw puzzle

Go to the hairdresser

Rearrange the furniture

Read a novel

Bake

Give/get a massage

Paint or draw

Study

Go to a sports event

Try out a new form of exercise

Go for a walk

Have sex

Enrol on a course
Go shopping
Volunteer
Write a short story
Call a friend
Grow plants
Write a comment on a social media group
Take some photographs
Invite someone to your house
Go to the cinema
Read a magazine
Write a journal
Give a gift
Clean out the fridge
Watch a film/documentary/TV series
Go to a concert
Set up a home spa with a bubble bath and face mask
Take the train to somewhere you've never been before
Go to a café
Do someone a favour
Go on an outing
Tinker with engines
Go to a bar
Make an item of clothing
Read something spiritual or philosophical
Meditate
Visit someone
Swim at the local leisure centre

Write into a newspaper
Masturbate
Go to a flea market or auction
Sing at home alone, with friends or in a choir
Do a workout video
Play video games
Try cooking a new dish
Go horse riding
Make cordial or juice
Donate to charity
Get dressed up
Borrow a book from the library
Go to a lecture
Go on a date
Review your finances
Go skydiving
Join a club
Take part in a religious activity
Join a book club
Eat ice cream in the park
Meet up with an old friend
Play football
Snuggle a pet
Flirt with someone
Play an instrument

You don't have to feel like it

Dreaming isn't enough. You have to actually do things. The biggest challenge here is that you probably don't feel like going for a post-work drink or making a healthy smoothie when you're feeling down (that's the problem to begin with). Just do it anyway.

This is why I recommend making plans. Schedule in meaningful activities that you continue doing regardless of temporary emotional dips. The best thing is to find feel-good activities that become part of your routine, such as an evening course or regular morning walks. That way, you don't have to stop every time and ask yourself if you feel like it. You simply do good things for yourself on autopilot.

Sit down and look at your plans for the coming week. Make sure you have things to look forward to, preferably something every day. It doesn't have to be big, maybe just calling someone you enjoy speaking to. Here are a few things to bear in mind:

- **Vary your activities.** Life becomes more susceptible to setbacks if you pin all your happiness on your relationship or job. It is common to feel helpless after a divorce because your partner represented not only your love life but your home, social life, evening routines and free time activities. Is it time to focus on other areas of your life that have been de-prioritised for too long (health, friends, leisure, family, work)?

- **Raise the bar gradually.** It's tempting to plan everything in at the same time. Sure, exercise five times a week is good for your health but this is an unrealistic goal if you're starting from the level of couch potato. Begin with something that feels appealing and achievable right now. You can always raise the bar again later.

- **Timing.** It's always best to plan in feel-good activities at the times when you might otherwise engage in 'feel-bad activities'. Are you in the habit of loafing on the sofa watching TV all night? Watching TV can be a feel-good activity, especially if you have a favourite show that you look forward to or watch with a beloved companion. But zoning out in front of the goggle box because you can't think of anything better to do soon becomes depressing. What else could you do when you come home exhausted from work? Indulge in a hot bath or take an evening art class?

- **Try out new things.** The world is brimming with entertainment, courses to take and societies to join, but you won't know what works for you until you try. Curiosity often comes more easily when you're in a good mood, so waiting to feel the urge before trying something new is a catch-22. A good rule of thumb is to try out an activity three times before writing it off as 'not for me'.

- **Get social.** Humans weren't designed to live shut up in individual flats with nothing but a nod to the checkout assistant at the supermarket every other day by way of social life. Try to find a social context where you can spend time with people. Maybe a club, volunteer programme or hobby. Preferably find people with whom you have things in common and meet up regularly.

Planning in feel-good activities is especially important during periods of your life that entail a sudden break from old routines and the need to establish new ones. Retirement, holidays, illness, having a baby, unemployment, moving to a new city . . . If you lose your traditional feel-good activities without finding replacements, you will soon begin to feel bad. Try to anticipate your needs, if possible. Before moving to a new town, look into what opportunities there will be to continue with your favourite hobby.

This became evident during the Covid-19 pandemic when society shut down overnight and many were forced to completely rearrange their everyday lives. Those who escaped their feel-bad activities, such as commuting and forced family reunions, found they had more time for their interests. Those who, on the contrary, lost their work friendships and chats over coffee, trapped at home with only hand sanitiser and jumbo packs of toilet paper for company, didn't have much to smile about.

Do it whole-heartedly

Your brain doesn't distinguish between sitting in the office or lazing on a sun lounger with a coconut drink in your hand. If you are dwelling on a work problem, you will feel tense and stressed regardless of where you are physically.

The same applies to the behaviour principle. In order for it to work, you have to commit to what you do. You're not going to enjoy any benefits of going to a party if you skulk in the corner on your phone instead of dancing or chatting. You could go to a thousand art galleries and have a lousy time if all you do is think *Why aren't I enjoying this? What's wrong with me?* instead of actually looking at the paintings.

Try to focus on what you are doing here and now. Do what you can to get yourself in the mood. You're not always in a party mood but you can help yourself get there by doing the things you usually do when you are in a party mood: put on some energising music, get out the party snacks and doll yourself up. In this way, you can create the conditions for yourself to feel other positive emotions as well, such as creativity or excitement.

I must emphasise that this isn't about faking a good mood. Don't force a laugh and pretend to be happy – that would only feel contrived and echo in the void inside. Let yourself feel what you are really feeling and make a choice to act differently. You can make an effort to see people even when you're not feeling smiley and bubbly. Be honest about how you feel. Say a colleague invites you out for a beer, you could always say: 'I'm not in a great mood today, so I might not be the best company. But if it's okay I'd like to join you anyway.' Sincerity usually feels better than fake enthusiasm.

It's not always easy to be mentally present in what you are doing. Maybe you're having lunch with a friend but no matter how hard you try, your mind keeps drifting away to a challenge you know you have to face later.

If you find it difficult to stay in the present moment, practising mindfulness can help. Conscious presence, or mindfulness as it is also called, involves actively directing your attention to what is happening here and now. Instead of engaging with every thought or feeling that passes by, you choose where to put your focus. This 'attention muscle' can be trained. There are plenty of apps and courses for people who want to learn some methods.

Now, of course, this technique won't work 100 per cent of the time. You might book a table at a fancy restaurant, dress up to the nines and do your best to keep the conversation flowing – but that romantic feeling just doesn't come.

Don't worry, it happens to us all. There will be other opportunities.

The behaviour principle is not a technique to force emotions. It is about creating the best possible conditions for desired emotions to arise. Invite them and hope they accept.

A word of warning: going over the top can be just as destructive as doing nothing at all. If the gap between what you feel like doing and what you try to coax yourself into doing is too big, it won't work. Imagine you don't feel like going to a party but push yourself to do so, get stinking drunk, and sing loudly and tunelessly in a desperate attempt to feign fun. Or you're having problems with your partner and don't feel much like romance, but instead of trying a quiet dinner at a local restaurant you go overboard on a decadent weekend getaway, fill the hotel room with heart balloons and propose . . .

Make sure you have things to look forward to, preferably something every day.

If you let the gap between what you feel like doing and what you encourage yourself to do grow too wide, it will feel forced. Start with small gestures and raise the bar gradually.

You cannot force happiness. But if you regularly

make space in the calendar and invite it, you will see that it starts to accept the invitation more and more often.

Outsmart your overthinking

The behaviour principle is not a panacea for unpleasant feelings, it is a method of managing those feelings to keep their frequency, intensity and duration to a minimum. Life will hit you with everything from loss and sickness to the person ahead of you in the queue buying the last doughnut. It is impossible to be happy all the time, you have to accept that there will be challenges as well.

Grief, for example, is a natural response to losing someone or something important to you. You can't avoid grief through distraction. Sooner or later, you will have to look the truth straight in the eye and learn to live with life's most difficult realities. That everybody dies. That terrible things happen to good people. That two people can love each other but still be better off apart.

When it comes to grief, it's recommended to take an 'alternating' approach. This means that you alternate letting yourself grieve with doing everyday tasks and feel-good activities to keep your strength and endurance up.

Anyone who tries to avoid difficult feelings at all costs is likely to make more issues for themselves. Ignoring problems often allows them to get worse. You might go around month after month with a vague feeling that something is wrong, a nagging feeling that won't go away. You are disappointed with how your life has turned out, with a dead-end job or loveless relationship, but instead of stopping and doing something about it, you escape into exercise or video games.

Don't avoid difficult thoughts and feelings. Remember to STOP – before you can employ the behaviour principle you need to make an honest effort to understand where the feelings are coming from and fix what can be fixed.

This is a delicate balancing act. Because there is a limit. Trying to understand your thoughts and feelings is not always constructive and can even become an emotion trap in itself.

I'm talking about brooding.

Brooding, or rumination, is when you get stuck in a negative thought pattern and can't break free. You spend your time turning over the same things over and over again in your mind: your relationship problems, decisions you regret, injustices you have faced, other people's opinions of you. It is also common to get obsessed with creating fictional scenarios that you then spend time resolving in your imagination.

Brooding is often about trying to understand why things are the way they are. You might, for example, become fixated on finding the root of your unhappiness. Is it childhood trauma, your partner's coldness, being bullied at school, your own mistakes and shortcomings? You think that if only you could get to the bottom of it, you could find the solution. Unfortunately, nine times out of ten, this way of thinking is a dead end.

Brooding is not the same thing as problem solving. Brooding usually focuses on the causes and consequences of problems rather than how to actually solve them. When attempting to solve problems, the focus must always be on finding practical solutions. It might feel like you're making progress when you brood but it's usually just a distraction to avoid actually dealing with your problems. The solutions you may come up with while brooding are rarely put into practice. You're much more likely to stay stuck in your head without doing anything concrete to improve your situation.

Brooding is also not the same as emotional processing. As I said, grief is a process of learning how to accept and live with new circumstances. Brooding allows you to keep living in denial, frantically trying to keep difficult but helpful realisations at bay by continuing to argue with them. 'What did I do to deserve this?' you may ask yourself over and over again. The answer is: nothing. Bad things happen to innocent people and there is nothing any of us can do about it. The real question is: how do you get your life back on track despite whatever awful things may have happened?

'What could I have done differently?' you might lie awake thinking. The answer is: lots. But you can't change the past. You have to make the best of the present and future.

Here is a trick to distinguish brooding from its more productive siblings – problem solving, processing and self-compassion. If you encounter an unpleasant thought and it is something you've thought about before with no fruitful outcomes, set a timer for two minutes. When the buzzer goes off, ask yourself whether you got any closer to solving the problem or gained any important insights in the last two minutes. If not, chances are, you're just brooding.

You cannot force happiness. But if you regularly make time in your calendar and invite it, you will see that it starts to accept the invitation more and more often.

This exercise can be difficult the first few times you do it but over time, you can get really good at spotting brooding.

The best way to overcome it is to get active. The brood mood thrives when you are lying idle on the sofa or in bed and feeling sorry for yourself. It's an emotion trap that will only make you feel worse – interrupt it by doing something else. Anything that isn't directly harmful and makes it hard to stay stuck in your head. Make a cup of tea, go back to your books. Get out your list of feel-good activities and choose something at random.

It won't help, your thoughts will resist. *You can't*

escape your difficult childhood/the futility of existence/ your boss's unreasonable demands. Ignore them. You're not good at problem solving when you're feeling low. Take the dog out for a walk and see if life brightens up a few shades.

Dream big

When you're feeling low, it's easy to go down the existential route and ask yourself the big questions. Who am I? Is this really how my life was supposed to turn out? What's the point of it all?

As far as I'm concerned, there is nothing wrong with the occasional existential crisis. Sure, it may be painful to take a hard look at your life and realise that you don't like everything you see, but I think it's a better option than just continuing to run blindly on the hamster wheel, only to regret all your missed opportunities in later life.

However, remember when I said that positive and negative emotions serve different functions? Feeling down makes it easier for you to spot problems and identify obstacles. Unfortunately, these negative emotions also make you lousy at actually dealing with them. It is when you are in a good mood that you see opportunities and have the energy to make changes.

You might think that the behaviour principle seems too simple to be effective in the face of real problems. And you would be right: you're not going to find a job or fix a marriage in crisis just by doing jigsaw puzzles.

You will need to address the underlying causes of your unhappiness, be it loneliness, relationship issues or a soul-crushing job.

But before tackling the big questions, it's often a good idea to cheer yourself up. You can only do a somersault on a bicycle once you have picked up enough speed and you can only tackle life's big questions when you have routines and pleasures that keep you ticking through everyday life.

Once you feel reasonably stable, then it's time to take a step back. What do you want in life? Really?

In modern Western culture, we often confuse happiness with success – a successful career, a desirable partner, exotic holidays and physical fitness. Put these norms aside for a moment and think about what happiness means to you. It might mean success in the aforementioned areas or it might be something else entirely. It could mean spending time in nature, contributing to society, enjoying your body or having intimate friendships. Are you happiest in company or spending time alone? Do you want to focus on your career or reduce your working hours?

How would you live your life if there were no expectations or social conventions getting in your way?

If you weren't getting in your own way?

If you wrote a bucket list of things you want to accomplish before you die, what would be on it?

Of course, the practicalities of life cannot be ignored.

Now might not be the best time to quit your job and move your family to the countryside to open a bakery. Or maybe it is! Either way, it is good to know what you long for deep down. Life is too short to stay stuck in situations where you're not enjoying yourself. Drastic changes in your life might not be feasible right now but it's almost always possible to take a step in the right direction.

How you get moving is the topic of the next chapter: motivation.

Supporting a Friend

Considering how common depression is (not to mention everyday low mood), you probably know several people who are struggling with a depressive emotion trap right now. Sometimes it is obvious. People can become sad and withdrawn. Others come across as grumpier and more irritable. Some wear a mask and laugh a lot but emerge from the bathroom with red, swollen eyes. What most people have in common is a tendency to retreat. They go into themselves, let messages go unanswered and stop engaging in things like they used to.

As an outsider, it can be difficult to know how to act. Should you check in or leave them in peace? Encourage activity or rest?

If you notice that someone is feeling low, you will get a long way by simply asking how they are and really listening to the answer. 'Maybe it's just my imagination, but you seem a little down. How are you doing?' is a good start. There is no need to offer solutions or profound wisdom. On the contrary, the simple act of sharing, not being left alone with their thoughts, can do a world of good.

You've probably gone through tough times yourself at some point and found that when you try to talk about it, people want to shower you with 'helpful' advice. Listening without interrupting or trying to make light of the situation is an art.

You might want to keep STOP in the back of your mind. Always start by showing compassion; empathise with how the person is feeling and why they are having a hard time. Only then can you help with thinking it through, examining different options and deciding what to put into practice.

The person in question may not want to talk, of course. In which case, you will just have to accept that. Tell them that you will be there if they change their mind.

Some take the agony aunt role too far and become the armchair psychologist of their friendship circle, workplace or family. This isn't a good idea for you or the person who is suffering. You can be an invaluable support as a friend or relative, but you cannot replace a professional therapist.

If you know someone who is very unwell or regularly needs to talk on the phone in the middle of the night, encourage them to seek professional help. You could even offer to be there with them when they call an advice helpline or make a doctor's appointment. If this person has concrete plans to take their own life, call 999 even if you promised not to tell anyone – most people feel grateful for the intervention when they feel better again.

Bear in mind that dwelling on your problems isn't always helpful. Just as thoughts can be divided into problem solving, emotional processing and brooding, talk can also derail into endless complaining. Encourage the person to express how they feel and what they plan to do about their situation but then switch the topic to something more pleasant.

I wish I had known this before I wasted countless hours in cafés moaning about hopeless boyfriends and incompetent bosses, instead of laughing and having fun with my friends. Or all the times my partner and I have tried to get to the bottom of a relationship problem, when a better solution would have been fewer awkward conversations and more evenings out at restaurants.

Step one: talk.

Step two: activate.

Depressed people aren't usually very interested in getting involved in fun activities. This is part of the emotion trap, so don't take it personally. But the more fun and meaningful things the person can manage, the better.

Encourage the person to stick to their routines. There is often a lot of resistance against, for example, going to work or the gym, but you usually do feel better afterwards (at least better than if you stayed home crying into a bowl of cheese puffs). It can be helpful to lend the person a hand with doing the dishes or making a difficult phone call, but you must also remember that the more the person does on their own, the more capable they will feel.

Advice is rarely appreciated. If I had a penny for every depressed client who had been advised to 'start working out!' I could buy a cruise ship and sail us far away from all the gym bunnies. Regardless of whether it is good advice, being nagged does not inspire motivation. Of course, this can be very frustrating for friends and family who are standing on the sidelines and desperately shouting advice, watching their loved ones sink deeper and deeper into the emotion trap.

Better to begin with encouraging activities that you know the person enjoys. Make plans together or offer to look after their children one evening so they can go to a gig, for example. You certainly shouldn't pressure people who are unwell but it's perfectly appropriate to give a friend a little extra encouragement when they are resistant. 'Come on, you don't have to be cheerful, it would just be great to see you there!'

Sometimes, knowing that your friends want to see you even when you're not at your best can be all it takes to brave the next step.

CHAPTER 3

Stop Waiting for Motivation

The Emotion Trap: waiting for motivation to come
The Behaviour Principle: getting started

On Motivation

We all wish for that movie montage. The Hero has worked through their yearning and doubts and finally made up their mind: scowling with determination, they tie a bandana around their head and take on The Challenge. They wake up to the clock radio flashing 6am, put on running shoes, hit the rain-soaked streets, jog up the stairs, trip over exercise equipment and give a friend (cheering them on with a timer in one hand and a doughnut in the other) a high five.

We dream of motivation. **Motivation** is that inner drive that pushes you to take action in pursuit of a goal. It makes it easier to get started, work harder and endure longer than if you were unmotivated. In short, it's a superpower that everyone wants. In psychology, motivation is usually divided into two types: intrinsic and extrinsic.

Intrinsic motivation is triggered by activities that are rewarding in themselves. You rarely need encouragement to do genuinely enjoyable activities – on the contrary, it can be hard to stop eating ice cream or playing video games until sunrise precisely because it feels so good. Strenuous activities can also trigger intrinsic motivation. For example, painting or programming can get you into a flow state, in which you feel utterly absorbed in what you are doing because you are stimulated and challenged.

Extrinsic motivation is triggered when an activity has positive outcomes. Going to work every day might not be fun but you get paid. Other positive consequences might be status, praise or avoiding the nagging of others.

Intrinsic motivation is sometimes considered 'better' than extrinsic motivation. In fact, we often perform at our best when we feel a combination of both types.

Intrinsic motivation makes it easier to focus on the quality of what we are doing because we enjoy the craft and our own skill development, but at the same time, internal motivation alone can turn into navel-gazing. An artist driven only by internal motivation would never show their creations to the outside world and a student with only internal motivations would get lousy grades.

External motivation helps us to adapt to our context and share our achievements. It often gives a greater focus on quantitative results, which can be acknowledged and valued by others.

The Emotion Trap

Motivation is as desirable as it is capricious. Sometimes, it graces you with its presence and you get a sudden urge to clean the kitchen. Other days, it doesn't make an appearance at all, no matter how much you poke and prod.

Lack of motivation can easily become an emotion trap. When you lack that drive, nothing gets done. You wait and wait but inspiration refuses to come. Days, sometimes weeks, go by and you begin to doubt your ability.

This affects your thoughts. Optimism and encouragement are replaced with harsh self-criticism: *I am so pathetic. This always happens. Why am I so lazy?* You invent all sort of reasons and excuses. You might sit for hours mulling over what is wrong with you.

This affects your emotions. The more time that passes, the more disappointed you feel. You become tired and listless, and motivation feels further away than ever.

All this negativity rubs off on your behaviour. To

numb feelings of guilt, you distract yourself with a thousand things – anything other than what you really should be doing. You procrastinate and postpone, immerse yourself in a TV series or find other ways to pass the time. One procrastination activity in particular is the most treacherous of all. I'm referring to the search for motivation.

Because lack of motivation is such a common problem, an entire self-help genre has sprung up focused on igniting that much-coveted spark. There are countless social media accounts with inspirational pictures and quotes. Lecturers who move us to tears with their uplifting life stories. Muscly influencers who build whole careers on roaring into the camera, telling you to pull yourself together. You can spend days chasing that spark, that impulse that will set you in motion.

There's just one catch: there is a psychological reason why these tricks don't work.

The Behaviour Principle

Intrinsic and extrinsic motivation have one thing in common: the reward only comes once you have started. It is only when you have become absorbed in activity that you can access feelings of pleasure and flow. It's only when you make progress that you can start reaping the rewards, whether that's bigger biceps or a cleaner kitchen.

Of course, you can also be motivated by hopes and promises of long-term results. You may have heard people singing the praises of the runner's high or have distant memories of it from your own flirtations with jogging, but it rarely becomes concrete until you actually feel it for yourself. And for that to happen, you have to get started.

When it comes to motivation, you employ the behaviour principle by taking the first incremental steps towards your goal. Even if you feel tired and uninspired. Even if your mind tells you that you're not good enough. Once you get going and start seeing results, motivation usually follows.

If you're lucky, you might occasionally be blessed with spontaneous motivation, but it isn't necessary to set the wheels in motion. On the contrary, an initial spark won't get you anywhere if the desired activity doesn't trigger intrinsic or extrinsic motivation. That's what keeps you going in the long run.

This might sound like a gimmicky rehash of Nike's slogan 'Just do it'. As I've said, if it were really that easy, you would have done it already. The behaviour principle is more about how to do it. How do you tailor a task so that it triggers motivation? How do you get started? How do you deal with setbacks?

Let me initiate you into the beautiful art of motivation cultivation.

OTHER CAUSES OF LACK OF MOTIVATION

Sometimes, your lack of motivation is a symptom of other emotion traps. In order to succeed, you will need to address the root cause of your troubles.

Feeling down? This chapter is about getting things done. When you are low, you often feel disinterested, tired and unmotivated to do most things (apart from watching TV and other escapes from reality). Read and work on the earlier chapter on joy and come back here when you have some energy.

Paralysed by performance anxiety or perfectionism? It's hard to get things done if you're terrified of making mistakes. This can be caused by unreasonable ideas of what you need to get started or the notion that everything has to be perfect before you can release it into the world. Read this chapter but also the next chapter on worry and anxiety to practise doing things to a 'good enough' standard.

What to Do

What is your goal – really?

Motivation is the drive to move towards a goal. This means that a goal is a prerequisite for motivation. Unfortunately, emotion traps tend to make us hopeless at goal setting. This can manifest in a myriad of ways:

- **Unspecified goals.** You feel strongly that your current situation isn't sustainable but are having trouble formulating a better alternative. You feel you should 'study more', 'get in shape' or 'take control of your life', but you're not sure exactly what you want or how to do it.

- **Unrealistic goals.** You stay up late frantically watching inspirational videos and promise yourself you will get up at 5am, do a hundred push-ups and make your dreams come true. When your 5am alarm goes off the next morning, one snooze is all it takes to abandon the whole idea.

- **Unappealing goals.** You look at what other people are doing and try to copy them. Even though you don't have any genuine desire to do weight training, or study medicine, or whatever it may be.

- **No goal.** You don't dare set a goal. If you don't have a goal, you can't fail! Genius!

Now I want you to be brutally honest with yourself. What is it you want to achieve?

And when you think you have the answer, I want toask you one more time: what is it you really want to achieve?

Mistake number one is setting a goal that doesn't actually feel all that appealing. A classic example is that you 'should' go to the gym and so you dutifully pay for an annual gym membership and never use it. Maybe your real goal should be finding a form of exercise that you genuinely enjoy.

Do you really need to be more attractive or is the actual goal to feel good about yourself?

Do you really need more money or is the actual goal to have a more enjoyable everyday life?

Do you really need to perform better or should your actual goal be to set more realistic expectations?

When you know what you want to achieve (or at least have a decent idea), the next step is to transform this vague vision into a concrete goal. You have probably heard this before – a good goal is SMART.

- **Specific.** Instead of a vague goal like 'study more', try to formulate something concrete such as 'three hours of studying per weekday' or 'to be able to answer all the study questions in the course book'.

- **Measurable.** To feel motivated, you need to be able to see your progress. Instead of 'eat less meat', your goal could be 'eat vegetarian three days a week'. This makes it harder to make excuses and easier to relax once you've achieved your goal.

- **Achievable.** What does your life look like right now? If you do shift work, have young children and live in a 'fixer-upper', following the exercise regime of a professional fitness influencer probably isn't an achievable goal (because they work full-time on creating their exercise videos and get daily support from their 100,000 subscribers). A daily walk at lunch and one good workout session at the weekend is perhaps more attainable. We perform at our best when our goal is challenging but within reach, so we know we can succeed if we put the effort in.

- **Relevant.** There are a thousand things you could be doing so you need to focus on what really matters. This can be especially challenging when a goal involves collaboration between several people. Setting a goal like 'spend more time with family' can lead to conflict if the other members of your family are currently prioritising work, hobbies or friends. Set common goals that are relevant to everyone involved.

- **Time-bound.** Why do you struggle to indulge in your passions while performing excellently at your boring job? We are spurred on when we are made accountable by deadlines (as long as they are reasonable). Book a trip to Tuscany for the end of your Italian course and you will be much more motivated to practise your language skills.

There are different types of goals depending on what you want to achieve. Let's say you are in a band with a few of your friends. You could set achievement goals (record an album), process goals (rehearse together twice a week) or learning goals (learn songs by heart).

If it's something you already know how to do and you just want to get going, achievement goals tend to get the best results.

If, on the other hand, you are starting something new, learning objectives might work better.

If you set the bar too high with a goal like 'write a hit song' when you don't know a guitar from a banjo, it creates tremendous pressure. You're tempted to skip learning the basics and become tormented by performance anxiety. 'Learn the five most common chords on guitar' could be a start or 'learn how to write a song'. Never written a book? Start by learning how to write a book.

DREAMS OF WRITING

As a child, I, like many people, dreamed of becoming a writer. I spent years daydreaming about all the books I would publish but, strangely enough, they didn't write themselves. I made some valiant attempts in a desolate Word document but it all came out as rubbish. I deleted everything.

It got to the point where I realised that if I really wanted to do this, I would need help. It took time to come to a decision but in the end, I put my psychology degree on hold and began a one-year writing course at a community college. Psychology could wait, I was going to learn how to write from the experts.

It was lucky that I already had half a psychology degree under my belt because as I sat there in my writing lessons, I couldn't believe all the myths spilling out of my teacher's mouth. 'You have to trust the process,' was the advice to students who had writer's block and were numbing their anxiety by binge-watching *Friends*. 'There is no right or wrong. This might be what you need.' They were clearly in the clutches of an emotion trap. And the teacher let it go on.

As for me, I had no idea how to write a book, so I read interviews with professional writers and a book on how to write a book. Apparently, one should consider writing as a job (if indeed you dream of it actually being your job and not just for fun). Done and done. I got up in the morning, brushed my teeth and went to the writers' lounge.

I kept busy for a few weeks. Months, actually. I wrote three pages a day and they turned out to be pretty terrible. Even my friends couldn't fake enthusiasm when I showed them.

Somewhere around Christmas, something clicked into place. I had pushed through the opening chapters of my novel and got to know the characters. They began to speak with their own voices. At some point in November, sheer exhaustion had rid me of the idea of how I 'should' write. Instead, I just wrote it all down as it came and the words flowed better.

My deadline was in June when the course ended. I had assigned one year of my life to my dream of being a writer and then it would be back to psychology studies. And though the chapters were slowly dripping out in October, they were positively gushing out by May.

I finished the damn book.

The manuscript was rejected by twenty publishers. How I got through the year of rejection letters is another story but in the middle of it all, a new Swedish publisher focusing on broad entertainment literature popped up. The book was accepted.

Yes, I was asked to rewrite the shoddy opening chapters, but the novel *Burn All Bridges* saw the light of day. And, believe it or not, it sold ten times more than the average debut.

Gamification

When you're stuck in the emotion trap of a lack of motivation, you often think that the fault lies with you. You are too lazy, undisciplined, have a bad attitude.

Why battle these unpleasant thoughts when you could simply make the task more motivating?

There is a reason why more than half of all Brits immerse themselves in video games from time to time.

Video games are ingeniously designed to hook the player. Skilled game developers have an understanding of human psychology and push all the right buttons to awaken our dormant motivation. They can make running a virtual bakery more fun than baking the same cake in your own kitchen – though only the latter results in something you can actually eat.

When you get stuck in the emotion trap of a lack of motivation, there is a lot to be learned from the world of video games. Let's look at a few common elements of **gamification** that you can exploit to make most everyday tasks more motivating.

Set short-term goals

Video games don't lure you in by simply presenting you with one end goal (rescue the princess). You are continually faced with shorter-term milestones (reclaim your sword from the orcs, find a travelling companion, seek out the wizard in the forest). When faced with tasks that seem complex and daunting, we quickly lose motivation. We are overwhelmed and don't know where to start. Following a curated path, on the other hand, where the next goal is just within reach, makes it easier to keep motivation up.

There is an art to setting good short-term goals. If it's too easy, you get bored and if it's too hard, you give up. The wonderful feeling of **flow**, when you become completely engrossed in a task, occurs when the difficulty level of the task matches your ability. It requires effort but you make continuous progress. You feel stimulated and competent.

Milestones can also help with **procrastination,** i.e. putting off tasks even though you know it will only cause you problems later on. Reading flyers or watering houseplants can suddenly feel urgent when you're trying to avoid a difficult task you don't know how to tackle. Do yourself a favour by making a proper plan.

If you want to break free from a lack of motivation, you need to begin by setting achievable short-term goals. Simple tasks that don't take too long so you can get the ball rolling and start seeing results quickly. It is better to set the bar low and raise it gradually than to set the bar too high and give up. This is something I often see clients struggle with in therapy. They are ashamed of never studying/having a messy home/not exercising but at the same time, they have too much pride to set a low-level goal.

You might occasionally be blessed with spontaneous motivation but it isn't necessary to set the wheels in motion.

The good news? The behaviour principle works well for this too. Even if you are embarrassed to set a low goal at first, the shame usually transforms into pride as soon as you see that you are indeed making progress in an area that is important to you.

So make a plan for your project. If you don't know much about the subject, the first step is to learn enough about it to make a sensible plan. Read a book, take an online course or invite someone knowledgeable for lunch to pick their brain.

If someone, such as a manager or teacher, has given you a task that you're not sure you understand, ask them to clarify. Remember: without a clear task, it is difficult to find the motivation to complete it. You can tell them I said so.

Let's say you want to declutter the basement. It's easy to lose your motivation as soon as you take a peek and get overwhelmed by all the chaos. Try to break it down into several steps – get moving boxes, sort things into piles, go to the recycling centre, arrange a yard sale – so it becomes more manageable. Each step can then be divided into further steps until you reach the point where each step feels doable.

You could start with a mini goal. A **mini goal** is something you can do to get started right now. It could be setting up your desk, booking a meeting or ordering the material you need. Easy wins in the beginning!

Just a word of warning. Planning is great . . . to a point. But there is a limit beyond which planning becomes procrastination. Don't spend forever reading, making detailed plans or choosing an essay topic. It's never going to be perfect. Decide how much time is reasonable to spend on planning and then move on to the next step, whether you're completely satisfied with your plan or not.

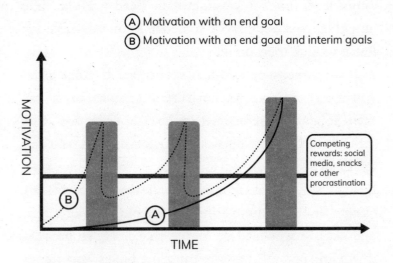

Feedback on effort

To have the endurance to keep going in the long run, you have to notice the progress you are making. You need to know that you are developing your skills or nearing your long-awaited reward.

In video games, you get feedback all the time. Every time you make the right move, you get points or encouraging whoops. When fighting an opponent, you sometimes have the luxury of a health bar in the corner of the screen that shows how much power each attack costs your enemy. You need never doubt whether you are on the right track or using the best strategy. It shows. Developing in this way and feeling competent is like an addictive drug for intrinsic motivation. However, the real world rarely provides such comprehensive feedback. It would be ideal if we could all have a wise mentor by our side, saying, 'That's right, keep going!' or giving us tips on how to optimise our efforts. If you're unlucky, what you might have instead is a manager with whom you only cross paths once a year at a performance review or one end-of-course exam for which you can only hope that you've studied the right things.

It is the concrete feedback that makes tasks such as cleaning or weeding a flowerbed so satisfying. You can plainly see how much dust has been sucked up by the vacuum cleaner and how shiny the mopped floor is.

When they hear 'feedback', most people think of criticism, but the fact is that encouragement usually motivates them more than reprimands. Knowing what you have done right, and what you should continue to do, leads to more and more things being done right over time. Think of a dog being trained to jump through hoops, encouraged at every step along the way with treats and praise. A dog that is punished every time it does something wrong will end up as a nervous wreck and stand there frozen in fear in response to being shouted at.

Constructive criticism can also be helpful, but it needs to be specific and well-meaning, and highlight something concrete that can be improved. Mockery and derision kill motivation. So the question is: how can you get feedback on your efforts? Do you have a mentor, study group or social media account that will allow you to showcase your work and get feedback? Can you get a smartwatch or exercise plan that will record your progress?

It can be scary to open up and ask for feedback. There is a fear of being ridiculed or criticised. Although this concern is often exaggerated, it may be justified – providing useful feedback is difficult and an art not everyone has mastered.

You can do a trial run by sharing something small that you don't really care about. If you get useful feedback, you can share more. If not, you can move on and ask someone else.

Biscuits in the break room

Why is it so difficult to save for a pension, lose weight or stop smoking? Because it's painful in the present moment (and therefore doesn't inspire intrinsic motivation) and the eventual reward is soooo far in the future (which weakens extrinsic motivation). If you're going to keep your energy up, you need to find carrots that you can dangle right in front of your eyes when you come up against obstacles.

Video games are usually teeming with rewards. When you clear a course, the screen explodes in a shower of confetti and you get better equipment, an extra life or unlock the next level. But in real life this can be trickier. In the workplace, for example, some employees work on commission, meaning they get paid extra for each deal they do. This is an effective way to increase sales – but, unfortunately, it can come at the expense of quality. In order to actually want to do good deals, and not just go through the motions like teenagers for their weekly allowance, what is needed is intrinsic motivation. This is best achieved through clear milestones, feedback and tasks that feel genuinely meaningful.

Treat yourself when you reach a milestone. If you've geared yourself up to make a difficult phone call and manage to do it, reward yourself with a fancy coffee at your local coffee shop. If you've completed a big project, treat yourself to lie-in or invest in some decent equipment. Choose something that suits you and your wallet. And make sure to switch between different kinds of reward so that it feels special and not routine.

Don't skip this step. Many of my clients shy away from celebrating – again, because they have a very high bar for when they 'deserve' to feel proud of themselves. Imagine if you had a boss who acted like that – whipping you to perform and then cancelling your promised bonus at the last minute. No wonder you lose your motivation! We need biscuits in the break room, after-work drinks and bouquets of flowers to keep that flame burning.

Another trick is to make the activity itself more rewarding. In psychological terms, this is called

temptation bundling, when you combine business and pleasure to increase intrinsic motivation. An example of temptation bundling is studying with friends because though the books themselves don't appeal, a gossip during the coffee break does. One American study managed to increase participants' gym visits by as much as 50 per cent. The trick? They were given an mp3 player with an audiobook of *The Hunger Games* that they were only allowed to use at the gym.

What could make your activity more attractive? Buying a coffee machine for the office, listening to your guilty pleasure podcast while cleaning the house or asking a friend for help in exchange for making them dinner? Be creative.

Make it easy to do the right thing

One of the challenges of low motivation is that distractions become so tempting. When the tax deadline looms it suddenly seems absolutely essential that you clean the windows. Countless office hours are wasted every day on news sites, mobile phone games and social media. If you are stuck in an emotion trap, you will probably blame yourself for this. You think that you are lazy, undisciplined and need to develop better willpower to resist temptations.

Then again, distractions are rarely a problem in video games. Super Mario doesn't get stuck watching YouTube videos. The football players in FIFA pursue the

World Cup without getting distracted by extramarital affairs. How come?

Because they can't! Unlike the real world, video games make it easy to follow the intended path – get ahead, talk to key characters, collect points. At the same time, it is difficult, sometimes impossible, to self-sabotage by going backwards or getting lost.

Instead of trying to adapt yourself, adapt your environment. Make it easy to do the right thing.

Some examples of lowering thresholds for the things you want to do:

- Get some stylish, comfortable workout clothes and keep them somewhere easily accessible.
- Tidy your desktop (both the physical one and the digital one) so there's no clutter beyond what you need right now.
- Fill the kitchen cupboard with snacks that are healthy and tasty.
- Choose the gym nearest to your home.
- Invest in decent equipment (but don't bankrupt yourself – start with the cheapest model and then upgrade later. The perfect reward for reaching a short-term goal!).
- Book yourself on a course.
- Clearly establish with your family the times when you aren't available.

Some examples of raising thresholds for things you don't want to do:

- Put your phone on silent and keep it out of reach. Decide on a time when you will look at it again.
- Choose a desk close to the corridor so everybody walking past can see if you're idly browsing the internet.
- Go to the library to study or somewhere else where there aren't too many distractions.
- Place a bet on yourself achieving your intended goal.
- Put a block on your bank card for online shopping.
- Uninstall distracting apps and replace them with better alternatives.

I have a friend who got through his studies by going home to his parents for a few weeks every exam period. Even though he was in his twenties, he found that he studied better with his father looking over his shoulder. Unconventional – but if it works, it works.

Get Started

Begin. Hopefully you should feel more motivated now that you have a clear long-term goal, some short-term goals, several rewards to look forward to and a plan to resist the distractions competing for your attention. Or maybe not. If not, take the first step anyway and follow through on your plan regardless of how it feels.

Touch the paintbrush to the canvas even if you don't feel ready. Keep going even if it doesn't come out perfectly. The same applies to going to the gym, clearing out the garage or writing an essay. It probably doesn't feel like much fun. And you might not even do a very good job, at least not at first. It doesn't matter. Keep going anyway.

As always, when you are working against the emotion trap, you will be bombarded with all sorts of negative thoughts. *This isn't working, I can't do it, I'm doing a terrible job*. Let them be. You don't have to argue with these thoughts or try to convert them into something positive. Just acknowledge them and don't be fooled into believing them. Turn your attention back to what you are doing and push on.

Maybe you can defeat the negative thoughts by doing the opposite of what they say. If your thoughts tell you to hide in a corner because you're too out of shape to be seen at the gym, stand right in the middle of the gym to do your stretches. If your thoughts say that there is only one way to write a good story, break all the rules of writing on purpose. Show your thoughts who's boss. They are good at making their voices heard but you are the one calling the shots.

The first time will probably be a struggle. And the

second time. But as you start to make progress, different thoughts and feelings are likely to come out of the woodwork. Perhaps you experience a burgeoning pride over actually getting started. Maybe you rediscover the pleasure of doing something that you used to love. Once you have got over the biggest hurdles – self-doubt and fear of failure – you will find the courage to experiment and that's when the real inspiration comes.

That is how you cultivate motivation.

Throw away the first painting that came out stilted and dull. Or frame it and put it in pride of place in your home. We can all do with a reminder that motivation comes to those who begin, regardless of how good or bad it comes out at first.

Refine your strategy

Sure, this all sounds great. But what if you've tried all the tricks and still can't get down to work?

Most life projects don't follow the Hollywood narrative of trying, succeeding and living happily ever after. For most people, motivation is something that comes and goes in rhythm with the ebbs and flows of life. You spring clean your whole house only to let it get messy again. You establish an exercise routine and then let it slip.

Don't lose faith. The point isn't never to fall, but to learn from your mistakes and get up again, wiser than before.

As you plan your project, schedule in points at which to evaluate and revise your strategy. At the beginning, follow-ups need to be frequent, preferably every week, so that you can recognise if you have started to veer off course early on. Once you establish methods that work, you can space out the evaluations.

Go back through this chapter and evaluate step by step.

What is your goal – really? Is this something that is genuinely important to you? For several years, I had a dream of being able to play the theme from the movie *The Piano* by heart. Two years of piano lessons later, I had got no further than 'Für Elise' and realised it was time to give up. It just wasn't worth it.

Maybe it isn't absolutely essential that you oil the garden furniture after all. Delete things from your to-do list rather than putting them off forever. Do you hate mowing the lawn? Divide your plot and share it with someone else or let your lawn become a meadow.

You might, on the other hand, come to the conclusion that this really is an important goal. Then you can think about your action plan.

- Have you made a plan with clear short-term goals?

- Are you getting feedback and support from someone else?

- Do you have attractive rewards to look forward to?

- Have you tried out all possible ways of making the work itself more appealing?

- Can you come up with more ways of adjusting the thresholds – low thresholds to desired behaviour and high thresholds to undesired behaviour?

If you have got this far and it still isn't working then you have two options: give up or seek help. This, after all, is why we live in a society – to help each other with important things that we can't achieve alone. Pick up the phone and call your boss, doctor or a charity helpline. We are waiting for your call.

Supporting a Friend

It can be frustrating to stand on the sidelines and watch someone you care about struggle to bring about change. They may have fallen behind in their studies, be battling challenges on the way to realising their dream or have a lifestyle that is going to cause serious health problems sooner or later. You try to encourage, reprimand and motivate, but nothing works.

To begin with, you must accept the harsh truth: you cannot change other people. They have to change themselves. You can offer help but it is up to them to accept it. Having said that, there are several ways to support a loved one who has fallen into the emotion trap of a lack of motivation. For starters, focus on the accelerator not the brake. Change often means both opportunities and challenges. It is all too easy for unmotivated people to get stuck focusing on the challenges. They dwell on how difficult everything is and all the things that could go wrong. It's like a car with the brake on; the accelerator won't have enough force to move it.

A common mistake is spending all your energy on removing the brake. You argue, complain and try to problem-solve. The person goes on the defence and just steps on the brake even more.

An alternative, which often works better, is to focus on the accelerator. The conversation technique **motivational interviewing** is performed by eliciting change talk – guiding the person to express ideas about moving towards their goal. Why they want this change, how it's going to work and what they are going to do when they get there. Forget the brakes! They tend to ease up on their own once the accelerator is strong enough. Listen, ask questions and encourage change talk.

'What inspired you to want to do this in the first place?'

'What a great idea! When are you going to do it?'

'How shall we celebrate?'

With any luck, this new focus of conversation will lead to an uplift in motivation. Encourage them to take advantage of it and get started right away! Together you might download a dating app, apply for courses, start an application . . . My favourite part of CBT is when I leave the room for five minutes and come back to an excited client who has finally made that difficult phone call.

For the spark to flare up into a sustainable flame, the activity needs to be rewarding – either the activity itself (intrinsic motivation) or its positive consequences (extrinsic motivation). Would it be more fun if you did the task with them? Maybe you could study or take on an exercise challenge together. Can you plan a really juicy reward for when the person finally achieves their goal? For example, a road trip when they get their driver's licence or a special dinner in their newly renovated kitchen.

Encourage and celebrate all progress. Unexpected rewards are often the most fun – a bouquet of flowers from your boss when you've been going the extra mile or a message from a friend who is proud of you.

You can also examine the thresholds in their environment. Especially if you are a manager, teacher, coach, parent or in some other way involved in the motivation of others. People tend to follow the path of least resistance. It's difficult for children not to get stuck in front of the TV if it has pride of place in the living room. And employees won't follow new procedures if it's easier and faster to stick to the old ones. Remember: low thresholds to desired behaviours and high thresholds to unwanted behaviours.

Sometimes, no matter how much you coax and prod, nothing changes. If your friend is dealing with a psychiatric condition such as alcoholism, long-term depression, substance abuse or gambling addiction, professional care is often required to deal with the problem. If they refuse to undergo treatment, there isn't much more you can do (unless it's a life-threatening situation, in which case people can receive treatment even without their consent).

Tell them that you will be happy to help if they ever change their mind, but then do what you must to protect your own wellbeing – even if it means cutting off contact. I repeat: you can offer help but it's up to the other person to accept it.

As always, when you are working against the emotion trap, you will be bombarded with all sorts of negative thoughts. 'This isn't working', 'I can't do it', 'I'm doing a terrible job'. Let them be. You don't have to argue with these thoughts or try to convert them into something positive. Just acknowledge them and don't be fooled into believing them.

CHAPTER 4

How to Reduce Worry and Anxiety

The Emotion Trap: avoiding
The Behaviour Principle: seeking out

It is difficult to say who was more terrified – me or my client. It was the spring term of my psychology degree and the crocuses were sprouting on the hill outside Stockholm University psychotherapy centre. After four years of preparation with heavy textbooks, role play and theoretical cases, I was now face to face with my first real client.

He wasn't feeling too confident either. After a few introductory sessions in which we had talked about his life in general, and how his problem had begun and developed, he was now facing his worst nightmare. He was only one metre away from a plastic tub containing a centimetre-long spider.

For those who do not have a spider phobia

(arachnophobia), it can be difficult to imagine all the issues these eight-legged creepy-crawlies might cause. It's more than just the shrieking panic on discovering such a creature in your home and begging a smirking family member to remove the monster. It might manifest as a state of hyper alertness on entering a room, having to quickly scan the mouldings and corners. It might cause shame to know on an intellectual level that this asphyxiating fear is, in reality, irrational. Or entail avoiding going up into the attic, having a picnic on a grassy lawn or visiting the relative you know has cobwebs in the bathroom.

Astonishingly enough, this type of terror, which may have held an iron grip on a person's life for decades, can in 80 per cent of all cases be treated during a single session of exposure therapy. This is when, under controlled conditions and in the company of an experienced therapist, you come face to face with your worst fear and finally learn to relax in proximity with a spider.

If the therapist knows what they're doing, that is. If, on the other hand, the therapist gets it wrong, it can intensify the phobia and leave the client more terrified than ever.

I swallowed and forced a smile, which I hoped was reassuring. It was time to get to work.

On Fear

Fear and anxiety get a bad rap. Maybe because we usually only talk about them in relation to the problems they cause. But the fact is, of all human feelings, fear is probably the principal reason for the survival of our species.

Fear is the body's alarm system. It is triggered when we perceive threat. It doesn't matter if it's a sabre-toothed tiger or a hostile person – the reaction is instinctive and lightning fast. Our pulse raises, breathing quickens and we start to sweat. The outside world disappears and all attention is focused on the threat. The number one priority is to ward off the danger either through fight, flight or freeze (i.e. playing dead).

This is an incredibly helpful reaction. It is what has protected us from wild animals and malicious neighbours over the course of human history. These days, it is what enables us to instinctively leap out of the way of someone speeding through a pedestrian crossing or hand over our valuables to a mugger without flinching.

Just as it's better for a fire alarm to go off one too many times than one too few, your internal alarm goes off in a lot of situations that turn out to be harmless because it's better to be safe than sorry. There is a distinction between **fear**, the body and brain's response to actual danger, and **anxiety**, which is the same reaction despite the danger being only imagined (or at least greatly exaggerated). Fear and anxiety feel the same but should be handled in completely different ways. We'll come back to that later.

Exactly what sets off the alarm is different for different people. There are certain triggers that seem to be hard-coded into human DNA because they have been a danger to our species throughout our evolution. Snakes, spiders, heights and social rejection are examples of things that most of us find uncomfortable. These are the most common fears to develop into phobia – i.e. a fear so intense and excessive that it interferes with everyday life. Of course, in modern society, significantly more lives are lost to cars, cigarettes and a sedentary lifestyle than these primeval dangers. No one screams in panic and demands that their boss remove unergonomic office chairs, although perhaps they should.

People tend to focus on negative information more than positive.

Other triggers are more unique to individuals. They come from negative personal experiences that have taught us to be wary so that we don't have to suffer the same trauma again. Someone who has witnessed a bank robbery might break into a sweat every time they walk into a bank. Anyone who has had their heart broken will find it harder to open up again.

Even when we are lying safely in bed, our internal

alarm can go off at the mere thought of future threats. Thinking about terrorist attacks (or simply giving a speech at a wedding) can evoke the same paralysing sensations as if we were actually facing danger. Just like the song that reminds you of your ex can bring up the same old emotions.

The sensitivity of this warning system varies for different people. There are some differences we are born with. Rumour has it that Barack Obama could have been confronted with a Declaration of War without so much as flinching. If, on the contrary, you are a neurotic person, your alarm might be going off almost constantly. A typo in an email can keep you up all night, worried about getting fired.

If your alarm is this highly sensitive, you might need medication to help suppress it. Alternatively, you could practise relaxation techniques so that you don't have to walk around with your body constantly at full tension.

FEAR
Reaction to real danger

Anxiety
Reaction to perceived danger

The Emotion Trap

I don't know what sets off your internal alarm system. Maybe it's needles, speaking in front of a crowd or using public toilets. But when the alarm goes off, it doesn't matter whether you're facing a roaring lion or a harmless house spider. It feels exactly the same.

Fear spreads like a poison through your veins. Palms become sweaty, muscles tense up. Your mouth goes dry, you get tunnel vision and hear your pulse throbbing in your ears. Your thoughts perceive everything through the filter of threat and it becomes difficult to evaluate the situation objectively, try as you might. *Did she just give me a dirty look? Why is my partner spending so much time chatting to that person?* You look for warning signals, the smallest signs that things might be going wrong. Your mind leaps to the worst-case scenario. *What if the spider jumps on my face, I have a heart attack and die? What if I suddenly feel sick and don't have time to get to the toilet before I vomit?*

Afterwards, you analyse what happened down to the smallest detail to assess any damage. You already start to worry about it happening again in the future.

Behavioural impulses are triggered to ensure your survival. Your movements become exact and alert. You may have a strong instinct to flee, just run away and not look back. You double- and triple-check that things are under control and ask others to confirm that everything is all right.

An intense reaction such as this calibrates the alarm system for the future. Unpleasant experiences are encoded in memory more strongly than neutral ones. This then causes the alarm to go off again the next time you find yourself in a similar situation or are reminded of the troublesome event.

If it's anxiety you're suffering from – not fear – this can really cause problems. Heart palpitations and sweat can be beneficial when you're facing an armed enemy, but less so if you're sitting in a restaurant wearing a pale blue shirt on a first date. The impulse to run and hide can get really awkward if what's freaking you out is a declaration of love or a credit card bill.

We all have our irrational fears and triggers. Personally, I have a very hard time with horror films, dishcloths and introducing myself in small groups. Most of the time, these fears don't really matter because they are not essential parts of life. As psychologists like to say: it's only a problem if it's a problem. But when anxiety and nerves start to prevent you from doing the things you want in life, it's time to act.

If you've been hurt, you may shy away from dating. If you hate the smell of hospitals, you may find excuses to avoid going to the doctor. Perhaps you dream of the next step in your career but are held back by performance anxiety, worry and nerves about job interviews. Your own body and emotions can feel like your biggest enemy. You feel blocked and trapped.

Once you start avoiding difficult situations, anxiety, like other emotion traps, can descend into a negative spiral. The alarm is triggered in more and more situations until you are in a state of high alert almost constantly. When I worked in a specialist clinic for severe anxiety disorders, many clients found it difficult to even leave the house without risk of a panic attack.

It doesn't have to be this way. There are ways to reprogramme the alarm. You can break out of your comfort zone and live life to the fullest.

The Behaviour Principle

There are lots of home remedies for people struggling with the emotion trap of anxiety. Some start with the feeling. You try to toughen up, pull yourself together, still your trembling nerves. This is usually about as effective as ignoring a blaring fire alarm.

Others try to tackle the thinking corner of the psychological triangle. You argue against your anxious thoughts, remind yourself that the risk is small. Unfortunately, your threat filter is usually good at finding counter arguments. Emotion trumps logic.

Then there is the third corner. Anxiety, worry and nerves can also be managed with the help of the behaviour principle.

In fact, this is the area in which the application of the behaviour principle has revolutionised my life the most. It has enabled me, someone who is at heart quite shy, to give lectures at international conferences and do live television interviews. I have even found the courage to tell waiters when the restaurant has got my order wrong.

The fire alarm can be recalibrated so that it stops sounding the alarm (or at least turns down the volume) in harmless situations.

What to Do

Tire out the alarm

What do you do if you have an overactive smoke alarm in your kitchen that goes off every time you cook? You probably don't sigh, shrug your shoulders and stop using the oven. The first thing you do is change the settings on the alarm. Similarly, you don't have to live with anxiety that prevents you from doing what you want in life.

What makes you nervous? Going to the dentist, being seen in swimwear, clowns?

Recalibration occurs when you apply the behaviour principle in anxiety-provoking situations. When, despite feeling nervous, you act against your impulses. Instead of avoiding, backing off, running away, you move towards, stick it out, hold your head high. You ignore the voices in your head telling you that your body shape is wrong for swimwear. You can acknowledge them but you don't have to obey them. Instead of hiding in the bushes as usual, you lay your towel down in the middle of the beach. When anxiety tells you to lower your gaze, raise it instead, stand up tall and try to make eye contact with the people around you (believe it or not, most of them will be taking no notice of you).

The alarm will still be blaring. Oh boy, will it shriek the first time you do it. Let it. An anxious reaction is hard work for the body, which doesn't like to waste energy unnecessarily. So when the situation turns out not to be so dangerous after all, the palpitations will slowly calm down. This usually takes anything from a few minutes to half an hour.

After this, you will have had a brand new experience. The situation wasn't dangerous after all. Even if it didn't go quite to plan – maybe a group of teenagers was sitting nearby and giggling for unknown reasons – the reality is very rarely as catastrophic as the horror scenarios you might have dreamt up beforehand. With the filter of threat over your thoughts, the smallest rustle in the bushes can be interpreted as a crazed axe murderer. Thanks to this success, your warning system won't sound as loudly the next time you find yourself in a similar situation. If you repeat the same thing several times, eventually the alarm will stop going off completely.

This technique is called **exposure therapy** and means deliberately exposing yourself to the cause of your anxiety in a controlled way. You battle against the instincts that tell you to flee and choose instead to stay in the situation until the anxiety subsides or the event is over. For this to work, the situation mustn't be too extreme – if you interrupt exposure when anxiety is at its peak, the alarm will get even stronger next time.

Exposure therapy can work wonders.

Once I cracked the code, I felt invincible. I've always been that person who sits by the bookshelves and reads at house parties. Suddenly, a world of new possibilities opened up. It was all just behaviour! I began to ignore the palpitations and blushes that occasionally flared up on my cheeks. I stopped listening to the negative thoughts that were pitching disaster scenarios in the back of my mind while I was going over to introduce myself to someone I admired. If I just behaved in the

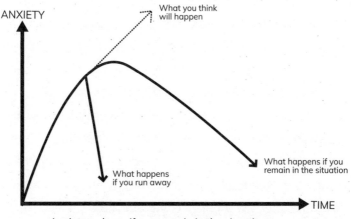

Anxiety reduces if you remain in the situation.

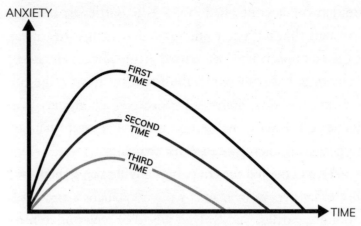

If you repeat the same thing several times,
anxiety levels will continue to drop.

ways I wanted to behave enough times it wouldn't be scary anymore. So that's exactly what I did.

What would you want to do if you weren't held back by anxiety and nerves? Say no, learn to salsa dance, be honest about your feelings? The first time you do something really nerve-wracking, like talking about your emotions, you will probably break into a cold sweat and want to run away. But the more you do it, the more natural it starts to feel. Until one day you can't understand why you ever thought it was difficult.

So, in situations that feel dangerous, I would encourage you to act in direct opposition to your instincts. Of course, this piece of advice has the potential to go very wrong. Remember that when you employ the behaviour principle to manage anxiety you must remember to STOP.

First, make sure you are practising self-compassion. *Don't be stupid*, you might say to yourself otherwise. *Stop being pathetic, just do it*. Remember that your reactions are a warning system shaped by evolution. They are based on inherited genes combined with the worst experiences you have had in your life. These are powerful instincts to go up against. Strive to treat yourself as an adult would treat a child, taking them by the hand to show them that there is no monster in the closet. It's okay to be scared – do your best anyway.

Second, you need to think. For starters, do you really want to do this? There is no point in fighting against your anxiety just for the sake of it. You can live a perfectly happy life without talking on the phone or jumping off the high diving board at the swimming pool. It can be liberating if there's something on the other side that is worth the effort, something you want to or have to do. Otherwise it's just self-torture.

And most importantly: is this genuinely dangerous? A horror story circulates among psychologists about the client who laid down on a country road in the middle of the night to overcome his fear of traffic, which he proudly told his therapist about the following week.

The behaviour principle should only be applied to situations that are basically harmless and where the fear is invented or greatly exaggerated. Asking someone out and being rejected might feel like the end of the world, but you will live to see another day. The same applies to fear of dying in a plane crash because in reality, the risk is vanishingly small. However, vigilance may be justified if a stranger calls and wants your bank details in order to pay out an inheritance that is as generous as it is unexpected.

How do you distinguish between rational fear and excessive anxiety? You could start by following the example of someone you know who seems stable and fearless without being reckless or often getting into trouble. How would that person act in this situation? Do what they would do.

My personal trick to determine whether it's nerves holding me back or something else is to visualise a red button. If I could press the button and have this unpleasant task magically accomplished already (the phone call made, the lecture delivered), would I press it? If the answer is yes, I go for it. Yes, it will probably feel uncomfortable but I am not going to let that stop me from doing what I want to do.

THE WORST THING YOU CAN IMAGINE

It started when I was eleven. I had just been watching an American TV show in which a teenage boy cut off his mother's hand. I lay awake for hours trembling. How could someone hurt their own mother like that?

What if I chopped off my mother's hand?

Once the image got stuck in my head, I couldn't get rid of it. What if I really did hurt my mother?

What if I murdered my whole family?

It was a horrifying thought and yet I couldn't shake it. I had read stories in the newspaper about people who suddenly lost their minds and murdered their entire family in cold blood. What if that happened to me?

I was terrified. And as the days and weeks passed, the fear began to spread.

I was terrified of knives – what if I stabbed someone? Terrified of traffic – what if I pushed a passer-by in front of a car? These thoughts haunted me everywhere I went and only got worse the more I tried to push them away.

Of course, no one could know. I would be locked up for life. Instead, I did everything I could to avoid being alone with my thoughts. I began reading constantly – while I was eating, on the way to school, constantly – until I couldn't hold my eyelids open any longer at night.

'How cute,' said the adults around me. 'She's become a bookworm.'

The nights were the worst. Everyone else was sleeping and there was nothing to stop me. I lay in bed with my eyes squeezed shut. I swore to myself that if I ever felt the urge to hurt people coming over me I would jump out the window. We lived on the eighth floor – it was high enough.

I became scared of windows too.

I didn't know it at the time but I was suffering from

obsessive compulsive disorder, or OCD. Obsessive compulsive disorder is a condition that involves being plagued by unpleasant thoughts you can't get rid of. These might be thoughts about causing accidental harm, like I had, that you are dirty or infected, or that you have to arrange things in a certain way. To relieve the anxiety, a person can get stuck in compulsive actions, repeating the same behaviour over and over again. For example, checking that the stove is off or excessive handwashing to get rid of imaginary germs.

Everyone gets intrusive thoughts sometimes. You might be crossing a bridge and be overcome by the impulse to throw your phone over the side or feel the need to tug on the door handle a couple of times to really make sure it's locked. This is normal and nothing to worry about. The problem occurs when you get scared. Then your alarm system might start to pick up on that particular thought. Your brain thinks this must be dangerous, something to keep an eye on. Ironically, thoughts that you try to force out with willpower tend to come back all the more because you are constantly monitoring them.

After a few years of peace, my obsessive thoughts struck again with full force when I was fifteen years old. I decided I would just have to risk imprisonment and I told my mother. Two months later, I was sitting in an armchair opposite a psychologist. Three months of CBT later, it was no longer a problem for me.

It was no picnic. The idea was that I had to expose

myself to things I feared in order to discover that the terrible thing would never actually happen. I didn't want to act on my thoughts – on the contrary, it was my worst nightmare. Letting all my horrible mental images run wild wasn't a pleasant experience but it worked. Three times a week I had to stand on the balcony and just wait to jump until I accepted the realisation that I was never going to do it.

The thoughts still pop up sometimes, especially when I'm stressed, but they don't scare me anymore.

Now I'm the psychologist who takes people by the hand and shows them the way out.

Raise the bar

When you start to face your fears, it's best not to set the bar too high. Especially in the beginning. Don't start off with your greatest fear. Not that it would necessarily be harmful to do so, but the risk is that it would be unpleasant enough for you to quit halfway through, thereby strengthening your internal alarm rather than weakening it.

Having anxiety isn't dangerous in itself. However, it can be extremely unpleasant. Your blood pulses in your ears, your heart races. When you're really nervous, it becomes impossible to sleep because your body is behaving as though you were trying to escape from a raging bear. It might feel like you're about to faint, suffocate or have a heart attack. Up to one in three people have experienced a panic attack, which is a sudden rush of anxiety when the fear caused by these physical symptoms escalates into panic.

What is happening here is that blood is drawn away from your hands and feet to accumulate in your large muscle groups. It can feel like you're about to pass out but in actual fact, you're far from it – fainting is usually caused by low blood pressure and during a panic attack your blood pressure is higher than usual. Hyperventilating can make it feel like you're gasping for air, even though you're actually taking in more oxygen than usual. Many people get chest pains, which can be mistaken for the beginnings of a heart attack. That's because your chest muscles are working hard when you hyperventilate, unlike the deep abdominal breathing you might do in a relaxed state.

All these symptoms are natural and harmless, but it takes a lot of discipline to simply tell yourself it's nothing, put on a smile and pour yourself a cup of tea. You can counteract these physiological reactions by trying to relax and breathe slowly, but that is easier said than done. Hence why it is best not to set the bar too high. In CBT, we usually rate exercises on a scale of one to ten, ten being the most stress-inducing for you, and tend to start with an intensity of five or six. Once you've got started and see that it works, it's easier to increase the intensity.

If possible, repeat the same exercise several times.

This will recalibrate your alarm more quickly. Dating coaching, for example, often starts with a phase of mass training, where the coachee has to go out and introduce themself to ten people at a bar, regardless of whether they are interested in them or not. This makes them more comfortable with taking the initiative and being rejected, without their alarms reacting as if it were the end of the world. It is also good to repeat the exercise at regular intervals, so the alarm doesn't revert to its previous settings.

Some anxieties can be difficult to get rid of precisely because they are experienced so infrequently. For those who are afraid of needles, having a vaccine shot every couple of years won't be enough. Why not accompany your friend who is a recurring blood donor? Appreciate the melodic pounding of your pulse in your ears – soon it will be a thing of the past.

BLOOD AND SEX

There are a couple of areas in which the behaviour principle must be used with care.

Blood phobia is one example. In normal cases, blood pressure rises when you feel anxious but in the case of blood phobia, it drops drastically. This is thought to be an evolutionary trick to guard against losing too much blood. To be able to expose yourself to blood without fainting, you first need to train in blood pressure-raising techniques.

Sex is another example. Few things kill a sexy mood as effectively as nerves. That's because sexual arousal is a result of both the sympathetic and parasympathetic nervous systems working in unison. If the sympathetic system goes into overdrive, for example because you are nervous or anxious, it can override the parasympathetic functions. The more stressed you become, the more desire eludes you.

Here, the solution is to stop pushing, pause and be in the moment. Instead of escalating sex, see if you can relax and do something you enjoy. Stay with it and don't move on until you feel like it.

Sometimes desire simply doesn't want to appear. Then it is important to stop and do something else. Make a bowl of popcorn and watch TV or focus on your partner for a while. Pushing yourself will only cause the alarm to go off again the next time.

Do the opposite

When we are nervous, we often come up with all sorts of tricks to calm ourselves down in the moment. These are called **safety behaviours** because they are things we do to make ourselves feel more secure when we think we are on shaky ground. People can get really creative here. It could be anything from avoiding eye contact and diving into your mobile phone like a security blanket to drinking whisky to calm your nerves.

It is difficult to say exactly what a safety behaviour

is because it differs from person to person. For some, it might be staying quiet, while for others it might be filling every silence with small talk. What all safety behaviours have in common is that they are emotion traps. Although they are employed to soothe you in the moment, they have the opposite effect in the long run.

Take jealousy, for example. Jealousy arises from the fear of losing someone who means a lot to you. These catastrophic scenarios are as painful as they are difficult to control because we can never fully know how another person feels about us or what will happen in the future. To calm these fears, you might resort to various safety behaviours that temporarily give a feeling of control. You ask how the person feels about you and your relationship. You pry into where they have been, who they've met and surreptitiously check social media to ensure no threats are looming on the horizon. In short, you obey your internal alarm system. You signal to yourself that this is a threat to be taken seriously and with the threat filter over your thoughts, every like on social media can appear as proof that the concern was justified. The consequence is that you may feel calmer temporarily but the alarm will go off even louder the next time.

There is only one way to recalibrate an overactive alarm system. Let the alarm continue to wail until it gives up and goes silent on its own. So, in the case of excessive jealousy, it is a case of surrendering, saying,

'Have a great time tonight' and then occupying yourself with something else, far away from your phone and its tempting social media feeds.

You could imagine anxiety as a monster that sits inside your head and tries to control your life. Every time you perform a safety behaviour, you feed the monster and it grows bigger and stronger. Not feeding it causes great suffering in the moment – the monster will growl and roar with hunger. But it is only by starving the monster that it will shrink and finally disappear completely.

Safety behaviours are the most common cause of exposure therapy not working. You go to party after party but feel just as uncomfortable every time. But look closer and you may realise that you are never really being yourself when you mingle – you avoid eye contact, rehearse every sentence in your head before you say it and only say what you think others want to hear. Or even worse: you sit in a corner scrolling on your phone. Instead of participating in conversation, you think only about how you look, sound and come across to others.

The behaviour principle is about acting as if you already felt safe. Only then can you realise that the terrible consequence you are so afraid of never actually comes to pass. Stop sucking in your gut, avoiding eye contact and triple-checking that you've done everything properly. You can do this!

Typical emotion traps linked to worry and anxiety

Area	Fear	Typical safety behaviours	Behaviour principle
Social situations	Embarrassing yourself	Planning what you're going to say in advance, scripting. Avoiding eye contact. Excessive politeness.	Maintaining eye contact. Speaking spontaneously. Relaxed body language.
Health	Serious illness	Googling diseases and symptoms. Checking for symptoms. Excessively seeking care.	Ignoring mild symptoms. Talking to a medical professional and taking their advice – no more, no less!
Jealousy	Abandonment	Interrogating your partner. Keeping an eye on their social media. Prioritising time with your partner over everything else.	Encouraging your partner to go out without you. Keeping yourself busy with your own interests.
Performance anxiety and perfectionism	Making mistakes and failing	Double-checking everything. Over-preparing. Spending far too much time on a given task.	Letting things go once they are good enough. Making small mistakes on purpose. Setting time limits for tasks.

Area	Fear	Typical safety behaviours	Behaviour principle
Appearance	Being rejected	Examining yourself in the mirror. Dressing to hide your 'flaws'. Erratic eating habits.	Wearing clothes you genuinely like. Going out without make-up/hair products. Eating at fixed times.
Accidents and disasters	Something terrible happening to you or someone you love	Double-checking the cooker is off and the door is locked. Asking people if something is safe. Calling/messaging just to check that everything is okay.	Checking the cooker/door once only. Following your own judgement. Getting in contact a regular amount.
Animals (spiders, snakes, wasps, dogs, cats . . .)	Being attacked	Finding excuses to leave the vicinity. Asking someone else to get rid of the creature.	Copying the behaviour of other people around you. Stroking pets. Reading/joining a forum for animal enthusiasts.

Experiment!

We all carry a lot of assumptions about ourselves and our environment.

If I step on a crack in the pavement, something terrible will happen.

I can only flirt when I'm drunk.

If I stopped bringing gifts, they would stop inviting me over.

Some of your assumptions are correct. Others are dead wrong. The sad thing is that you are probably carrying around a lot of completely false assumptions that are limiting you in your everyday life and getting in the way of things you really want to do.

Are you holding on to any assumptions that you suspect might not be true? Test them out and see!

In CBT, testing the validity of your assumptions by deliberately acting in a new way and seeing what happens is called a **behavioural experiment**. Just like a scientist, you formulate a hypothesis beforehand (if I buy condoms at the pharmacy, the cashier will laugh at me) and decide how likely you believe this horrible consequence to be (75 per cent).

In the name of science, I've picked my nose in supermarkets, sat in cleaning cupboards and faked panic attacks on the bus. And you know what? So far, I have never been laughed at, died from lack of oxygen or been arrested. It was an eye-opener for my client who was watching from the sidelines and plucked up the courage to try it themselves.

After saying the wrong thing on purpose a few times, you are no longer as anxious about speaking in front of people.

What assumptions are limiting you?

Interrupt the thought ping-pong

When you are frightened or anxious, it affects your thoughts. Even in our normal state, we humans already have a **negativity bias**, i.e. a tendency to focus on negative information more than positive. This makes it easier to survive but, unfortunately, harder to live. We focus more on what goes wrong than what goes right, interpret ambiguous information pessimistically and feel more sad to lose something than happy to gain something of equivalent value. This is why you might have a hard time remembering all the encouragement you received at your last performance review but can recite the criticism word for word.

Any threat that might be looming on the horizon further reinforces the negativity bias. A threat filter settles over your mind and awareness of danger becomes your highest priority. You find it difficult to focus on other things. You start playing out all possible and impossible scenarios in your head and you overestimate the likelihood of them happening. It's easy to get caught up in worry (thinking about possible future threats) or brooding (repeatedly going over things that went wrong in the past).

Worry often manifests as a game of mental ping-pong. On one side of the table, you have your Logical Self asserting that everything is going to be okay, that you are capable, that the house probably won't burn down just because you forgot to unplug the kettle.

On the other hand, there is your Frightened Self looking for weaknesses in this logic and listing everything that could possibly go wrong. 'But what if this happens? Or this?'

It's difficult, maybe even impossible, for your Logical Self to emerge victorious from the match. Your Frightened Self doesn't abide by the rules and can defy both the laws of physics and common sense. Fear of a monster lurking under your bed, waiting for you to stick your foot out from under the cover, is far-fetched, to say the least. Still, why risk it? Every reassurance can be followed by another *but what if?*, which means your capacity for worry is as infinite as the human imagination.

A little bit of worry is good sometimes. Worry stops us from throwing ourselves headlong into new situations, encourages us to consider risks and take reasonable safety measures. However, the threat filter makes it easy for worry to get out of hand. It overestimates the risk that you will be laughed at, reprimanded or become the victim of a zombie apocalypse. Then, because thoughts influence behaviour, it can also lead to unreasonable safety behaviours. You double-check, over-prepare or even back out altogether. You become absent at the dinner table because your mind is preoccupied with the worst events of both the past and future.

How do you know where the line is between appropriate and excessive concern? Here again you can use STOP to help you. Think about it – is this train of thought helpful to you? If the answer is no, put an end to it. Cancel the mental ping-pong match. Forfeit the worries. Refuse to get sucked into the argument.

When the worry thought comes: 'But what if this happens?' just answer: 'It might happen. We'll see,' and focus on what you need to do. Cook a carbonara, play with the kids or do something else that feels meaningful to you.

This is obviously easier said than done. Worries will bombard you for a while longer. But they need fuel to keep going. If you manage to refrain from debating with them and just leave them hanging, they tend to shut up eventually.

Train yourself to focus your attention by practising **mindfulness**. Notice your thoughts and feelings without getting wrapped up in them. Instead, you keep gently guiding your attention back to the present moment.

The practice often begins with directing your attention to a specific sensory impression – for example, your breath. Every time your attention flutters away is an opportunity to centre it again. When you have got good at this, you can start to consciously direct your attention to other things, such as what you are doing at the moment. You can be consciously present while doing the dishes, going to a restaurant or having a job interview. It takes a couple of weeks but most people will notice a difference after practising mindfulness for just fifteen minutes a day.

Maybe you have dabbled with mindfulness at some point and it wasn't for you. Mindfulness is a bit like cardio – it's beneficial for everyone but there is a myriad of methods out there and you might have to try different ones to find the right approach for you.

You can also use 'mindlessness', i.e. distracting yourself. Instead of carefully redirecting the attention away from the worry, you overpower it with other stimulations, such as listening to a podcast or turning on the TV. This is an effective strategy but it has its limitations. Distraction works well if the worry is temporary – say, you just want to get through the evening. If, on the other hand, the worries are constantly recurring, distraction can become a lifestyle where you are constantly keeping yourself busy to avoid confronting troublesome thoughts. Some people try to block out suffering by immersing themselves in work, video games or partying. It can help if the distraction actually fixes the problem (for example, seeing friends if you're feeling lonely) but otherwise, it usually just defers the problem to later.

When you feel bad, always start with STOP. Why do you feel the way you do right now? Is there anything you can do to fix the problem? Talk to someone who can help you find solutions.

If you often find yourself distracted by idle pastimes,

use the chapter on joy to identify your feel-good activities. Something that feels genuinely rewarding. It's a shame to go through life distracted. If it is difficult to cope on your own, consider seeking professional help.

Expand your comfort zone

'Do one thing every day that scares you.' This is a common piece of advice. Sounds like a massive pain if you ask me.

There is no intrinsic value to fighting your fears. Everyone is afraid of things and that's okay. It might be worth battling through your nerves if there is something worth gaining on the other side, but there's no point in doing it just for the sake of it.

I'm afraid of the dark and know exactly what I need to do to rid myself of my fear. But given how rarely I'm home alone, it's not really worth the trouble to crawl into the closet and wait for the hands of death to grasp my neck (hands that I intellectually understand will never come). However, it is important for my life that I am able to give lectures, meet clients and go to the supermarket with unwashed hair. So I do. No matter how much my worrying thoughts protest.

By the way, my first exposure session went great. Mostly.

Contrary to what many arachnophobes believe, house spiders cannot jump. They're also not interested in crawling up your nose or getting tangled in your hair. However, the little rascals can leave cobwebs in their wake, allowing them to apparently fly through the air on invisible strands, seeming to defy the laws of nature.

I was as surprised as my client was when this happened. In the second it took me to react and capture the spider, my client had made it halfway out into the garden and was writhing in disgust in the crocus bed.

If our session had ended there, his continuing treatment would have been an uphill struggle, as his alarm system was now screeching louder than before. But my client was brave and, after a few deep breaths, managed to come back inside. We completed the session and he felt very proud of himself.

Exposure therapy doesn't always have to go completely according to script. On the contrary, it is often beneficial to 'fail' sometimes. Tell a joke that falls flat. Request something and be turned down. Resit an exam. First of all, failure actually occurs less often than you expect. Then, when it does, you almost always manage it better than you think you will. You realise that the things you have feared, the things that have been holding you back all these years, aren't that big a deal after all.

If you woke up tomorrow and all the nerves holding you back were gone, what would you do?

'Do what you want to do every day – even if it scares you.' I think that's a better motto.

Supporting a Friend

If someone reveals a fear to you, you should feel honoured. It is something we usually only share with people we trust because it exposes vulnerability.

When we share our worries the last thing we want is lectures or advice. We want validation – confirmation that our experience isn't weird, wrong or unreasonable, that it's understandable to feel the way we do in that moment. Half the job of a psychologist is to validate people's experiences (the other half is to revise them, which is not always as popular). There is no need to agree that the experiences are objectively 'correct'. Nor to agree on how the situation should be handled. However, you can always demonstrate that you understand the other person's perspective and empathise with what they are going through.

Teasing, mocking or dismissing fear damages trust. The worry is still there but the person will continue to hide it from you to avoid being ridiculed.

Our first impulse is often to try to fix the problem. Though this comes from a good place, it is often better to ask how the other person intends to handle the situation themselves first. They will usually have their own ideas for solutions and just need an energy boost to muster the courage. Meddling with unnecessary problem-solving risks making the person doubt their own judgement and feel even more insecure.

Sometimes, it doesn't matter how much you talk, reassure and problem-solve – it won't help. Your friend has set you up as their opponent in mental ping-pong. 'But what if this happens?' they ask. 'I know it's unlikely but what if it doesn't work?' As I said, worry's counter-arguments are as unlimited as the human imagination, so the match can go on forever. You can spend hours dissecting a problem to death without getting any closer to a solution.

Do what you want to do every day – even if it scares you.

If you have a friend who easily gets caught up in worry and brooding, do them and yourself a favour by pausing the game. Change the subject or occupy them with something that makes it difficult to ruminate at the same time. If the person's mood improves, the threat filter will often remove itself from their thoughts. Problems are usually easier to deal with after an evening filled with laughter than one filled with anxiety.

There is only one way to ease the anxiety once and for all: to recalibrate the alarm system. To go against the worry and uncertainty and actually act, even if it's uncomfortable. You can support a friend through this by cheering them on, encouraging them and celebrating progress together. You can recommend this book and talk to each other about which problems you want to support each other to overcome.

Pick your battles. Sometimes putting up with each

other's pet peeves is a part of friendship. Some prefer not to talk on the phone or take the bus alone. As long as life goes on and everyone is happy, there's no need to change. But watch out for signs that support is descending into co-dependency, when a reassuring word is no longer enough and your friend or relative finds it difficult to make simple decisions or complete everyday tasks on their own. They might expect you to check that the stove is off, show your chat history to prove you've not been unfaithful or accompany them out of a shop to get a breath of fresh air. This can go so far that you become a crutch that the other person cannot do without.

You are doing your loved ones a disservice if you adopt these safety behaviours. Even if it helps in the short term, it can make the problem worse in the long run. It rarely helps to refuse – often the person is so anxious and upset that it will only create an argument. But do talk it through afterwards and try to find a better way to handle similar situations in the future.

Encourage the person to seek professional help. You can offer to make an appointment and accompany them the first time if that makes it easier to get started. You could ask to see the therapist together and focus the session on how you can help support your loved one's treatment.

Even if the person doesn't want to get help, and would rather continue with their emotion trap, be clear about your boundaries. They have needs but so do you. You shouldn't have to be available 24/7 or listen to the same rant for hours if it makes you feel bad. It can feel tough, especially if you've been a reliable crutch until now. But this very thing, the realisation that their emotion trap has extended to affect the people they love, can often be the wake-up call they need to get to grips with their problem once and for all.

CHAPTER 5

On Stress – Work Smarter, Not Harder

The Emotion Trap: work harder
The Behaviour Principle: work smarter

It was the final day before the deadline. I was due to start a new job on Monday and I had to submit my manuscript to my publisher. I was typing so fast that the keys were practically bursting into flames. I had been up half the night comforting a friend whose cat had been taken to the emergency vet. It also happened to be the very same day that my publisher's catalogue was going to print and I wanted to cry when I saw the press images.

My phone rang. It was the guy I had been dating for a couple of weeks (and who I'd managed to completely fall for already) saying he thought we were moving too fast and he wanted to take a break.

Fine, whatever. I didn't have time to feel sad about it. Back to work.

I sat down in front of my computer and continued

tapping away. It was strange – I got a distinct feeling of déjà vu. Had I already written this section? I scrolled through the text. No, everything was as it should be. Weird.

I carried on writing but the feeling just intensified.

I was supposed to send the manuscript in for feedback. Who was I supposed to send it to again?

As I sat there staring at the screen, it felt as if my surroundings were slowly starting to disintegrate. What was I doing? Where even was I? I tried to get a hold of my thoughts but they slipped away like sand through my fingers.

Was I having a stroke?

The Body's Natural Energy Drink

Stress is the body's natural energy drink. It is a primeval response that garners your strength and equips you to face challenges. The body and brain's resources are redistributed to make you alert and strong. It might be in response to a physical challenge like lifting something heavy or a mental challenge like staying awake.

To put it simply, you might say that the body's stress system is divided into two branches: the sympathetic nervous system (the accelerator) and the parasympathetic nervous system (the brake).

When you are confronted with a threat, activity increases in the sympathetic nervous system. The body's energy is mobilised for fight or flight. Your pulse increases, your blood flows away from the digestive system and into the large muscle groups. You become tense and restless, and your breathing becomes shallower. The brain also changes gear; you become alert and your senses are sharpened. The mind focuses fully on the threat at hand and how to avert it.

It is something of a simplification but it is generally believed that people perform at their best under a moderate level of stress. This is illustrated by an inverted U curve known as the Yerkes-Dodson law. At the bottom of the curve, when you're swinging drowsily in a hammock without a care in the world, you perform poorly. If someone gives you a difficult maths problem you'll probably just blink in confusion.

With just a little bit of pressure, you become sharp and focused. You get fired up and ready to exert yourself. But if the stress gets too intense, you become over-excited and get tunnel vision. The blood goes from the frontal lobes to the more 'primitive' parts of the brain and you find it difficult to think clearly.

Under extreme stress, your brain switches over to a fight or flight response – you panic. Panicked people are rarely efficient.

There is a limit to how long the body can continue expending energy. Just as a battery needs to be recharged, the human body needs recovery in order to endure in the long run.

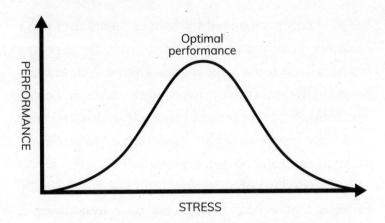

When the danger is over, the body's 'brakes' take over. The parasympathetic nervous system calms and restores balance to the body. It resumes de-prioritised body functions such as digestion, wound healing, reproduction and sleep.

In other words, stress is a good and useful response. It gets you ready to handle challenges and live a rich life full of bustle and activity. Provided that you regularly recover, both physically and mentally.

The Emotion Trap

This is where we risk falling into the emotion trap. Our biological programming assumes that the threat we face is as temporary as an attacking hyena. Once the danger is averted, we get our much-needed rest. Alternatively, the threat is as serious as a prolonged famine – it depletes our resources but the only alternative is death.

In modern society, we are faced with different types of demands. We struggle with ongoing issues and ever-growing to-do lists. Not only are we expected to perform at work, but other parts of life – home, physical health, relationships – can feel like demanding projects too. There is nowhere to rest.

Stress settles over your thoughts. You get tunnel vision and find it difficult to assess situations objectively. Stress is all you can think about, all tasks feel urgent and it becomes easy to overestimate their importance. In reality, it probably isn't the end of the world if you fail an exam or your partner is disappointed in you – but it might feel like it.

Your emotions keep you going. You become tense, restless and frantic.

Your behavioural impulses soon become unsustainable. Pick up the pace, press on, work harder, do more . . . Breaks are often the first thing to be pushed to the sideline when you're in a hurry. On the off chance that you do manage to get a breather during the day, you might use the time to make a call or catch up on a few emails. These are strategies that work in the short term – for example, if you only have a few days left until a deadline. But as a lifestyle over months and years, it's the perfect recipe for stress-related illnesses.

The parasympathetic body functions cannot remain on standby for an indefinite length of time. If the digestive system is de-prioritised for a long time, you can get stomach problems. Persistent muscle tension leads to aches, high blood pressure and even cardiovascular disease. Your libido decreases because your body is set to survival mode, not survival of the species. When your mental resources are exhausted, you become unfocused and suffer from memory problems and a short temper.

Have you ever noticed that you get sick more frequently during stressful periods? In the short term, stress strengthens the immune system. But if you stay at a high level of stress for an extended period of time, your immune system takes a beating and every little cold hits you hard. Or some people don't get sick at all – until the first day of their holiday. One hypothesis is that this is a result of rampant inflammation, which the immune system doesn't have the resources to deal with until you relax.

If you recognise yourself in several of these symptoms, it may be a sign of a chronic stress problem. And if that is the case, then you need to act now because if you continue in the same vein there is a serious risk that you will burn out. Contact your doctor.

Some people make a distinction between positive stress – i.e. challenges that feel fun and exciting – and negative stress – i.e. things you feel compelled to deal with. Positive stress can be, for example, a new job or a date that you are looking forward to. From a physiological perspective, however, they affect your body in the same way – regardless of what is making you stressed, you need recovery time to manage in the long run.

Some people brag that they never get stressed and are resistant to burnout. This is just as absurd as claiming you can run indefinitely without rest. Some people are fitter than others and some are more stress-resistant, but everyone has a limit.

When you are in the middle of the emotion trap of stress it can be difficult to get out. Maybe you've tried to wind down with relaxation exercises but felt twitchy about the annoying sound of dripping water in the background. Perhaps a well-meaning friend has urged you to 'Relax!' and you've had to suppress the urge to headbutt them.

Don't worry, there are things you can do. We are about to go through some methods of dealing with stress using the behaviour principle.

What to Do

Take a break

The first thing to fall by the wayside when you're stressed is the breaks. You skip lunch and scowl at your colleagues laughing merrily in the break room. This is a lousy strategy and I'll explain why.

If you do strength training, you will know that you can handle more repetitions if you take regular breaks than if you try to do them all in one go. The same applies to running – you can run for longer if you pause to catch your breath every now and then. This is exactly how it works with mental effort: you need rest to endure over time.

The human brain is not built to stay focused on one and the same task for several hours at a time. After an hour or so, your mind starts to wander, whether you like it or not. You can push yourself to continue, force your attention back to the task at hand, but it takes more energy.

Ironically, work without breaks often takes longer than work with breaks because you have to compensate for your decreasing productivity as time goes on. Furthermore, when you eventually finish, you feel as limp as a wrung-out dish cloth. So breaks do not mean that less gets done. Quite the opposite.

You can probably think of an example of a time when you've wrestled with a seemingly unsolvable problem only to crack it the minute you leave your desk. Stress gives you tunnel vision on the task at hand and limits your capacity for associations and creativity whereas you become an expert in this kind of thinking when you have the opportunity to relax and daydream.

In addition, when you come back from a break and look at your task with fresh eyes, you may find that you have got too stuck in one way of thinking. You reorient yourself in the task, standing back to take in the broader view that you lost when you buried yourself in the work. There might be a more efficient way to approach it that ultimately saves time.

Of course, this doesn't mean that your lazy colleague who seems to be playing around on their phone all day is the most productive person in the workplace. Breaks are effective between periods of work, not as a substitute for work. But we also shouldn't fool ourselves into thinking that the people who work through lunch and read emails during meetings are necessarily the most efficient.

Thus it is important to take breaks in general. Both in the short term (during the day) and the longer term (weekends and holidays). How you take breaks is also important.

To really disconnect during your breaks, you need to do something else. Preferably a different activity in a different environment. Switching tabs on the computer from one task to another is not an optimal break. Nor is getting up from the meeting table with colleagues and sitting down at the coffee table in the next room.

Good breaktime activities might be watering plants or walking the dog. If you have a sedentary lifestyle, it can be nice to stretch or take a walk around the block, though this might be the last thing you want to do when you're feeling the pressure. Your stress reaction is constantly telling you to go back to the task at hand, that you have an enemy to defeat before you can relax. But you know better. I often say that the inbox is like a hydra – cut off one head and two new ones will appear in its place. Breaks will increase your endurance in the long run.

Being idle and spending time alone with your thoughts can be painful. Literally. In one study, people were left to sit alone in a room for a short time, between six and fifteen minutes. They could choose between sitting and thinking or giving themselves electric shocks. If you've ever noticed how many people pick up their phones as soon as they find themselves standing in a queue, you'll know what the results were. Half the men and a third of the women chose the electric shocks.

This condition is somewhat jokingly called paxophobia – a strong aversion to relaxation and peacefulness. If you recognise yourself in this, it is a sign that you need to take breaks more than ever. Schedule breaks in like you would important meetings.

Stress is the body's natural energy drink.

The sort of breaks people need depends on the individual but start with the assumption that you need to briefly stretch your legs every hour and take a couple of longer breaks if you exert yourself throughout the day. If daydreaming over a cup of tea isn't for you, run an errand or do the dishes.

You also mustn't wait until you're already exhausted before taking a break – this lengthens the recovery time necessary to get back to workable energy levels. It's better to take short breaks preventively. Don't let yourself be tricked by excuses like 'but I'm in the flow now'. Being in the flow now is great but staying in the flow for the rest of the day is better.

This also applies to people who have problems with procrastination. Many procrastinators think they aren't entitled to breaks after taking so long to get started in the first place. In fact, the lack of breaks can in itself be a cause of procrastination. You will be less inclined to get started if you know that you're embarking on a marathon session until dusk. Take breaks on schedule (the motivation chapter earlier explains how to break a marathon into manageable milestones).

Resist the urge to fill every micro-break with activity. Instead of manically scrolling social media or checking the news while waiting for the bus, take a few deep breaths and look around you.

Work smarter

When you're stressed, pausing and relaxing helps, but it's rarely enough. The problem remains: I have too much to do and too little time. How do I solve this seemingly impossible equation?

Very simply put, stress management can be divided into two different categories: active and passive coping. **Passive coping** occurs when you see yourself as a victim of circumstances. You struggle, suffer and try to dodge extra responsibilities. However, you do nothing to actually change the situation. **Active coping** is about trying to fix the roots of stress once and for all. For example, by finding a more efficient way of working, trying to push back a deadline or asking for help.

For example, let's take the stressor of your inbox being flooded with newsletters that you don't have time to read. Deleting the emails or moving them to a folder called 'Read later', where they remain unopened until the death of the internet, would be passive coping. Active coping means opening the emails, scrolling down to the bottom and clicking 'unsubscribe'.

Active coping often takes longer in the moment. However, it saves energy in the long run because it solves the problem permanently. What strategy do you think the emotion trap drives us to?

When you are stressed, the behaviour principle is about seeing past your stress behaviours (work harder) and replacing them with more long-term stress management (work smarter). You know better than I do what challenges you are facing and what passive or active coping would mean in your situation. But let's go over some common pitfalls and see if any of them ring true for you.

PITFALL 1: Multitasking instead of monotasking

When you're stressed, you might be frying sausages, helping the children with their maths homework and booking a haircut all at the same time. You are saving time by doing several things concurrently. Or so you think.

Multitasking is when you engage in two or more activities at once. It feels like you are focusing on several things when in fact the human brain can only focus on one thing at a time. However, what it can do – and do very well – is switch focus quickly. The brain can switch focus so fast that it feels like you are thinking about several things at once. However, this ability comes at a price. It takes mental energy to switch between activities, to constantly reorient oneself. You will end up feeling more tired and stressed than if you do one thing at a time.

There are some activities we can do simultaneously because they are simple or automated. We can iron or drive a car while listening to the radio because the movements are carried out unconsciously. But as soon as something unexpected happens that requires your focus, you stop paying attention to what you're listening to.

Your friend sitting opposite you replying to a text and claiming that they are still listening to you? Lies! It might be a case of self-deception but it's lies all the same.

This means that when it comes to tasks that require focus, you work most efficiently when you work sequentially. Instead of attending a lecture and fiddling with other things at the same time, finish what you're fiddling with first and listen to a recording of the lecture afterwards (maybe while ironing?).

If your task requires focus, try to eliminate all distractions while you work. Close unnecessary tabs on the computer. Put your phone away. Hide at the library to escape family chaos at home.

The best thing I ever did for my own efficiency at work was turn off email notifications. In three clicks I went from constant interruptions to undisturbed harmony. I check my emails twice a day – before lunch and in the late afternoon when I'm too lazy to concentrate anyway. If that doesn't feel reasonable in your circumstances, what would be appropriate? Challenge your emotion trap – you probably don't need to check them as often as you think.

If you don't have the opportunity to work undisturbed all the time at least try to have some focused work sessions. Maybe you can work from home a couple of days a week?

PITFALL 2: Cracking on instead of planning

If you are short on time, you don't want to waste precious minutes on planning. Unfortunately, such short-sighted thinking can cost you many unnecessary hours in the end. For example, you may spend several working days reading about physiological reactions to stress, only to realise that the text you're writing doesn't need to be longer than half a page anyway. To give a completely random example . . .

When you feel like you are drowning in stress, it's time to take a step back. Plan what you're going to do and in what order. To-do lists can help but they can easily become tangled thickets of tasks that make it tempting to start with the simplest jobs just because they're easy to cross off. Create an overview by writing subheadings: Today, Tomorrow, This Week and When Possible. Get into the habit of going through your to-do list and removing anything that has been sitting there for months without action – it probably wasn't that important to begin with.

One way to get an overview can be to book focused work sessions into the calendar. If you estimate that a task will take two hours to complete, schedule it into your calendar just as you would schedule a meeting. This is a great exercise for people who tend to overwork tasks. Practise submitting your work when the time is up, even if it isn't perfect. With a little practice, you can settle for making things good enough.

To combat stress, it is important to make your plan realistic. You can't be Super(wo)man every day. Include breaks, setup time between meetings and some wiggle room in case Karen from finance asks for some emergency IT help. One really good tip is to start the day with the most important task, when your brain is freshest. Then your tasks will just get easier throughout the day.

When you see your plan in black and white like this, it can sometimes become painfully clear that you simply can't do it all. You have to cut down on your commitments. Which leads us to the next strategy: boundary setting.

PITFALL 3: Saying yes instead of setting boundaries

It is easier to say yes than no – in the short term. You avoid potential conflict, long discussions and disappointed faces. The headache comes later when you actually have to make good on your promises.

Here, your clear planning will come in handy. If, for example, you work part time and it becomes clear that your responsibilities cannot possibly be fulfilled within your working hours, take a list of your tasks to your boss and ask them which ones should be prioritised and which should be removed. If they are recurring tasks, they probably need to be delegated to someone else, rather than you failing to do them every week.

Practise saying no to extra commitments. Do it next time you are asked to attend a meeting, organise the Christmas party, visit your great aunt Mabel or anything else you have neither the time nor inclination to do. 'No, unfortunately I'm fully booked at the moment.' 'No, I'm sorry, I don't have the time.' 'No, not this time. But thanks for asking!' If you're the kind of person who tends to say yes on impulse, only to suffer anxiety when you see how full your calendar is, say you will get back to them. Don't commit to anything without consulting your diary first.

Saying no can bring up all sorts of unpleasant imagined scenarios. What if your client gets angry, your family thinks you are ungrateful or your friends never want to invite you again? Ask yourself how you perceive people who protect their boundaries. A polite but firm no can cause frustration in the moment but you probably respect people who show this kind of integrity. And I bet you appreciate this behaviour a lot more than people who procrastinate, under-deliver or flake at the last minute because they never really had the capacity in the first place.

The first thing to fall by the wayside when you're stressed is the breaks. You skip lunch and scowl at your colleagues laughing merrily in the break room.

It is a good idea to take a step back and examine your commitments in general. Do you have certain tasks that you really dislike and that someone else could do instead? Perhaps it is worth hiring a cleaner or giving up your role as parent football coach.

Do you make demands on yourself that get in the way of what is really important to you? Try inviting your friends over for dinner without vacuuming first and serve up frozen pizza instead of a home-cooked meal. Is it really such a disaster after all?

PITFALL 4: Doing everything yourself instead of developing a support network

Another common impulse when you are stressed is to do everything yourself. That way, you know for sure that the children's PE bags are packed or the warehouse items are stacked correctly. Plus, it's quicker than explaining to someone else how to do it, you tell yourself. If someone else attempted it, you'd probably have to clean up their mess afterwards anyway.

There is some truth in this. When you delegate tasks and get help from other people, it is unlikely that the tasks will be done exactly the way you want. If it comes down to individual tasks, it may be worth the effort to simply do it yourself. But when they pile up, not asking for help soon becomes an emotion trap.

Try to create systems that don't depend on you to function. You never know, something might happen to you. Being the only adult who knows the children's schedule or the only employee in the office who knows how the laminator works makes the whole system fragile. If something were to happen to you, someone else needs to be able to step in. You can get used to someone else doing the washing up badly. Trust me – I learned that one the hard way.

Of course, collaborating can be easier said than

done. Arguments and misunderstandings can arise. One excellent method that works in most contexts is team debriefing.

Team debriefing is a method for developing co-operation in a group. It is often used in workplaces but it works just as well in families, associations or relationships. At a team debrief, you sit down and evaluate previous collaboration. This can be done monthly, when you finish a project or after a bad night out. Ask yourselves:

- What worked well, which we want to continue doing?
- What worked less well, which we need to find another solution for?
- What could we try doing instead?

When you sit down and evaluate your caravan holiday, you might note that everyone was good at double-checking they hadn't left their phone behind after every stop. And it worked well when half the group prepared the dinner while the other half assembled the outdoor tables. However, the terrible argument on the approach to Margate was not a highlight – next year we'll have an emergency stash of bananas in the car to ward off blood sugar dips. Also, preferably fewer booked overnight stays so there is more time for spontaneous swims.

If you have regular debriefs where you focus on

finding solutions (rather than pointing the finger at scapegoats), collaboration usually flows better over time. Studies show that it can improve the productivity of a work group by as much as 25 per cent!

I still consider one of my greatest professional achievements to be when I managed to squeeze the weekly meeting down from ninety to fifteen minutes, through the power of recurring debriefs. Fewer sighs and eye rolls and more time for coffee.

PITFALL 5: Postponing the problem instead of solving it

Few things cause as much stress as slow-burning problems. Long commutes that eat into your free time. Money worries. Conflicts with a colleague that never seem to end.

When stress becomes so strong that it is over-whelming, a common reaction is passivity. You feel powerless, weary and see no way out. You lie awake at night mulling over the problem – not how to solve it but how things turned out this way. Alternatively, you try to avoid thinking about your problems altogether. Regardless of strategy, the result is the same – you do nothing to solve the actual problem.

Of course, sometimes you are hit by extreme life circumstances where you can't actually influence the outcome. You may have been notified of a serious illness or be waiting for a response to a job application. But in most circumstances, there is something you can do to improve your situation. Doing what you can, however small, can counteract the emotion trap of stress. It replaces fatigue and powerlessness with resilience and growing self-confidence.

Here, I will outline a problem-solving technique that is often taught in psychotherapy. It can seem silly in its simplicity but it is actually one of the most powerful tools there is for improving your mental health. The trick is to actually use it.

1. **Define the problem.** Being unhappy or dissatisfied with your job is too big and vague, try to formulate the problem as concretely as possible. For example, 'I want to make new friends to hang out with on the weekends.'
2. **Brainstorm solutions.** As always with brainstorming, don't censor yourself. Even ridiculous suggestions can be helpful because they might give you a laugh and humour helps you break out of the tunnel vision of stress. Write at least ten suggestions. For example: join a club, invite colleagues over for dinner, take a course, reconnect with my ex, invite my anchovy-smelling neighbour over for coffee.
3. **Evaluate the suggestions.** Once you have written down all the solutions you can possibly think of, go through and evaluate them. Cross out anything illegal or inappropriate. Weigh the

pros and cons of the best suggestions. Maybe
you really can't handle that anchovy stench
after all.

4. **Choose one solution.** Maybe you're not sure
whether it's going to work but it's the one that
seems the most doable. Even if joining a club
has never really appealed, it can't hurt to try.

5. **Make an action plan.** If it's hard to get moving,
take another look at the chapter on motivation.
What is the first step you can take today? For
example, you can look up three different club
meetups and put them in your diary.

6. **Evaluate the result.** You can only evaluate the
result once you've given your chosen solution
an honest attempt. Did it work? Great! Or not
so much? Then start again.

Stress can feel overwhelming, but try to resist the pull of
the emotion trap to run, hide, or put up with it. You don't
need to stay in an unsustainable situation. By doing what
you can to manage it, feelings of stress can be reduced.
Step by step, you regain control over your life.

Limit limitless work

I spent time working in a private therapy clinic. One of
my clients was a middle-aged construction entrepreneur,
father of three, haggard appearance. He told me that he

had been feeling unwell for a long time and it was all linked to stress. He felt hounded, inadequate, and he couldn't stop thinking about work, even at the dinner table with his children.

This was illustrated by his phone going off every five minutes during our conversation, at which point he would excuse himself to make sure it was nothing important. Even during our therapy session, he wasn't putting his mental health first.

We booked the next session for two weeks later. In the meantime, I asked if we could do a little experiment. He would turn off his ringtone and email notifications, and he wasn't allowed to check his inbox at all after working hours. He was sceptical but he was paying for my advice after all. He agreed to try it out.

Two weeks later, he appeared with a badminton racket in hand and looked ten years younger. He

You mustn't wait until you're already exhausted before taking a break – this lengthens the recovery time necessary to get back to workable energy levels.

muttered somewhat sheepishly that he probably didn't need therapy anymore. He had stopped being available 24/7 and started exercising again. Business was going well and he felt like a new man.

This might sound unbelievable – stress management isn't always this simple. But sometimes it really is.

In order for you to get the recovery you need, it's not enough to leave the workplace physically – you also have to disconnect from it mentally. Just because you can take work with you up a mountain or into bed doesn't mean you should. Modern working life can make working from home feel more like living in the office.

It may seem impossible, but you can use the behaviour principle to create mental boundaries between stress and recovery time.

1. PLACE

Just as your brain has learned to associate hospitals with ill health and the smell of cleaning agents, cues in your surroundings will remind you of either stress or relaxation. Having a place to go for work or study makes it easier to focus on the task when you are there – and to let go of these thoughts when you leave.

When you are not at work, try to rid yourself of any reminders of work. Remove the work email icon from your phone's home screen. If you wear work clothes, change as soon as you get home. Don't work in your dressing gown because not only does this take home comforts to the office, it also brings the office to your weekend comforts.

This is especially challenging if you work from home. Ideally, you should have a place where you only ever sit to work – and never (ever!) work in bed. If you sit at the kitchen table make sure you clear away any stress triggers before you start eating.

You can also use various rituals, such as taking a short walk at the beginning and end of the working day.

2. TIME

Working during office hours, even if you are studying or have flexible hours, can make a big difference. You know when you start and can allow yourself to mentally clock out at 5pm. This allows you to avoid that constant nagging guilt that you should be working. It also makes collaboration and family life easier when the people around you are used to a predictable schedule.

Of course, sometimes there are good reasons to work evenings and weekends. Or so I've heard. In which case, it can be helpful to set limits by planning a work shift in advance, say from 9pm to 10pm. Before and after are free time. If work ideas pop up outside working hours, they can be noted and deferred to the next planned session.

3. AVAILABILITY

If a pinging phone has become background music when you're chilling out on the sofa, it will be difficult to relax. Turn off notifications from as many apps as possible. Hide work emails in a folder that you only check during working hours.

Have a conversation at work and around any other

commitments that you need to take a break from sometimes. What expectations of availability can you agree between yourselves? It is common to overestimate how quickly you are expected to respond – especially outside of office hours. If you are expected to be reachable at all times, this should be considered on-call time and should be reflected in your pay.

Resist the temptation to 'just quickly check your email' at 10pm. Opening your emails to calm your worries is a crystal-clear emotion trap.

4. TALKING

If your stress levels have been rising steadily all week, it feels good to get it all off your chest over a glass of wine on Friday night. Your incompetent boss, IT frustrations or clients' unreasonable expectations. Talking about how you're feeling is good, as we know, but bear in mind that, from a psychological perspective, thinking about work counts as unpaid work time. If you continuously dwell on the same topics, this is passive coping – you relieve the pressure without addressing the underlying problem. Go back to the previous section and see if there is any way you can solve the problem once and for all.

There is always more to do and our emotions are excellent at reminding us of this. Setting boundaries between work and leisure can often feel uncomfortable at first. Feelings of stress can rise temporarily because you're plagued with thoughts of everything that could go wrong. Push through. Just like when you use the behaviour principle in other contexts, the voice of stress usually quietens down after a while.

So, you've suddenly found yourself with lots of free time. What the hell are you going to do with it?

Worker ant or playful grasshopper?

When someone says 'recovery', the first thing that comes to mind might be collapsing on the sofa with your feet up. The idea that recovery is synonymous with physical rest is probably a hangover from the time when most people had physically demanding occupations. After a long day in the fields, rest is what you need most of all. Those of us who have sat slumped in an office chair for eight hours, however, need to recharge our batteries in completely different ways.

Just as we have different muscle groups, we have different types of fatigue. We have mental fatigue after concentrating for a long time on complex problems. There is also emotional fatigue when we have been sociable and considerate of others all day. Physical fatigue comes from physical exertion. And finally, we have sleepiness that creeps in when we have been awake for a long time.

Different types of fatigue require different types of recovery. Binge-watching TV on the sofa is excellent recovery when you are physically tired because your body gets a chance to rest. Mental fatigue, on the other hand, can be dealt with by going for a walk or pottering around the garden. If you've been working hard to be polite all day, a bit of solitude can do you the world of good.

Fatigue	Recovery
Mental	Dinner with friends, exercise, gardening, dancing, sex
Emotional	Solitude, spending time with a close friend or pet
Physical	Watching TV, reading, taking a bath, playing video games
Sleepiness	Sleep

This is where the emotion trap can set in. There are many emotions that can be confused with fatigue: low mood, disappointment, boredom . . . If you come home after a long day at work, salsa dancing may be the last thing you feel like doing. You would probably prefer to collapse on the sofa and not move until bedtime. Rest is tempting because it doesn't require any effort – but it doesn't necessarily refresh your energy levels either.

What does recovery mean to you? Which activities, interests and relationships give you renewed vigour and energy? I really doubt that watching TV while scrolling on your phone is the answer, even if that is how you tend to spend your evenings. What could you do instead?

Paradoxically, exercise can be one of the best forms of recovery – at least, if you have a sedentary job. Exercise, especially cardio, causes the sympathetic nervous system to kick in just as it does during stress. When the workout is over, the body's brakes are automatically activated to flush away the stress hormones. You rarely feel as relaxed as after a solid cardio session. If you exercise regularly and build up your fitness, your body will get used to the activation of the sympathetic nervous system and won't find it so demanding, even when you are stressed about work. Exercise makes you more stress resistant.

Still not convinced about the importance of free time? One American study, which has become a modern classic, followed forty American scientists throughout their careers. In the 1950s, when the study began, they were all promising young academics. When the study was completed in the 1980s, two groups could be discerned from among the participants. The first group had reached a plateau in their careers. They held respectable positions as researchers and teachers, but their careers were nothing compared to group number two, which consisted of highly successful scientists who had exceeded all expectations and made breakthroughs in their fields. Some of them had even been awarded the Nobel Prize.

At first glance, it was difficult to see what differed between the two groups. All participants were intelligent and hard-working, but when their free time activities were taken into account the answer became clear. The more successful scientists tended to have more leisure interests. They devoted a lot of time to art and exercise, and valued activities that they considered enriching. Those whose careers had stagnated had fewer interests, were less physically active and believed that spending more time working was the only way to get more done.

The idea that we have to choose between productivity and fun, being the ant or the grasshopper, is a false dichotomy. We feel and perform at our best when we combine the two. The best days and weeks are varied.

However, a word of warning. Social pressures can push you to strive to fill your time with accomplishments (successful career, well-behaved children, training like an elite athlete, a home that could be photographed for an interior design magazine at any given moment). Demanding leisure interests can be restorative – for example, it is difficult to dwell on work stress while playing football. But if you're having a stressful time, think about what is really going to allow you to recover. Spending your holidays writing a novel or renovating the summer house might not be appropriate if it feels like more of a duty than a hobby.

Sleep

Prolonged stress often leads to sleep problems. Which is hardly surprising, considering that stress triggers the body's fight or flight response. You wouldn't wonder why it was difficult to relax and go to sleep right after being chased by a rhinoceros. Yet, physiologically speaking, this is exactly what many people do when they stay up half the night preparing a presentation then go to bed exhausted but worked up. The body's accelerator is still going. You toss and turn in bed and have difficulty letting go of stressful thoughts. If you do manage to fall asleep, you wake up two hours later with palpitations.

Everyone has troubled sleep sometimes. And suffering a few bad nights during a particularly stressful period won't cause you any long-term harm. If you maintain your usual sleep routines, your body will compensate for the lost hours with an increased percentage of deep sleep or a longer sleep on the weekend. However, persistent sleep problems cause problems.

During sleep, the body repairs itself. The brain is active too, clearing out waste products, processing the day's events and putting memories into storage. In other words, sleep is essential to sustained functioning. Emotion traps can trick you into compromising on sleep but that is a dangerous, slippery slope. Lack of sleep makes you more sensitive to stress and lowers performance – which you may have to compensate for by working even more hours. If sleep continues to be a problem, it's only a matter of time before you burn out. If this is the situation you find yourself in now, I urge you to make an appointment with your doctor.

Every individual has different sleep requirements.

Most adults feel alert after seven to nine hours of sleep. If you function well in everyday life and don't feel sleepy during the day, you are probably getting enough sleep. How alert you feel immediately upon waking is a poor measure of how sleepy you are. The neurotransmitters of sleep can linger in the brain for some time, so it is normal to feel sluggish when you wake up.

Caffeine is the stress junkie's best friend. Remember that even if your much-anticipated caffeine kick only lasts for half an hour, the half-life of caffeine in the body is about four to six hours. That means if you drink six cups of coffee spread throughout the day, you still have two or three cups in you by bedtime. Not great for sleep.

Alcohol often makes it easier to fall asleep. However, the sleep will be lighter and generally less restorative than if you go to bed sober.

It is common to have trouble sleeping on Sunday night, as many people take naps on Sunday. One way to avoid stumbling to work like a zombie on Monday morning is to try to keep roughly the same bedtimes on weekends as during the week. Daytime parties and early movie marathons are underrated.

Sleep well!
You can help to regulate your internal body clock with a few basic ground rules.

- Try to keep regular sleeping hours by going to bed and getting up at approximately the same time every day.

- Exercise and make sure you see daylight during the day, especially in the morning. This helps to regulate your body clock.

- Deal with stressful things during the working day, then devote the hours before bed to relaxing activities. Read a book, drink herbal tea, soak in a bubble bath. And for god's sake, don't check your emails at bedtime.

- Help your brain associate bed with sleep. If you can, watch TV or study anywhere else other than bed. Go to bed only when it's time to sleep.

- Put your phone on airplane mode or leave it in another room so you won't be tempted to use the internet during the night. If you have trouble sleeping it's usually better to read a book than to have literally all the entertainment in the world at your fingertips.

Supporting a Friend

It can be very difficult to break free from the emotion trap of stress on your own. You get stuck in tunnel vision and find it hard to take a step back and reassess the situation. Just like the frog that stays in the pot as the temperature slowly rises to boiling point, you take your stressful everyday life as a given and neglect to act before it's too late.

We have learned that stress is caused by a combination of unreasonable demands, inadequate handling of those demands and inadequate recovery. You, as a friend or relative, can support a stressed person with all three of these issues. Let's start with the demands.

Anyone who works in a hectic environment can easily develop a distorted perception of reality. They consider it reasonable for their boss to call in the middle of the night to yell at them or that it falls to them to make up for someone else's flawed planning, time and time again. You can provide a grounding in reality by pointing out that this is not normal, that there are alternatives and that something has got to change.

However, people stuck in the emotion trap of stress are rarely interested in advice. They like to vent about how stressful everything is but ignore suggested solutions. They are too busy with passive coping to have energy for anything else. Here, you have to start with empathetic listening and show that you understand how tough the situation is. Of course, if there were an easy solution they would have already tried it.

Only when you have shown that you understand the situation can you start discussing solutions. Ask them what they think first; they probably have ideas. Is there anything they can do to sort out the situation once and for all? Encourage them to get to the root of the problem. This could be done by talking to their manager (again), looking for a new job, switching to a cheaper car or something else.

Offer help. Maybe you can run errands, look after the children or help in some other way until the situation calms down? Is there anyone else you can call in to help? Becoming someone's crutch is unlikely to be sustainable in the long run as it will only enable them to continue in the same stressful rut. But temporarily giving someone the breathing space required for active coping is often valuable.

The same applies if your boss is having a tough time and keeps expecting you to step in and cover for them. It may be a temporary solution but it won't last in the long term. Take it up with your boss and if nothing comes from that you may have to take the issue over their head.

If you live with someone who is feeling stressed right now, you probably need to sit down with them and discuss your commitments. Who will take care of what? Maybe you will agree to a temporary unequal split of chores to help them out but, if so, define how long that will last. It's easy to dismiss problems by saying 'things will get easier soon'. But life is happening right now and no one should have to put up with living in a fog of stress, with one person bearing all the responsibilities for home and family.

Addressing the stress is step one. Step two is often much more pleasant: taking time to recover.

Encourage your partner to start jogging again. Invite your friend out for a beer. Offer to babysit for parents of young children so that they can have a few hours of peace at a restaurant – even if you all know perfectly well that your babysitting efforts are going to end up with the living room smeared with half a bottle of ketchup.

When you're hanging out and having a good time, agree not to talk about what's making you stressed. And if you do, keep it brief. Both put your phones away and focus on something other than the chaos in your lives right now.

We all have stressful periods. It's normal and nothing to worry about – as long as we get the recovery we need. Look out for signs that stress is starting to get out of hand. Such signs might include difficulty sleeping, uncharacteristic mood swings, concentration and memory difficulties or eye twitching. Then it's time to pull the emergency brake. A change is required to prevent your loved one from burning out. Encourage them to seek professional advice. This will enable them to review their situation and find better ways to deal with unhealthy stress.

CHAPTER 6

Eight Common Challenges

Congratulations! Hopefully you now know a little more about how to use the behaviour principle in practice – especially to help boost your self-esteem, motivation and joy, and reduce anxiety and stress.

Maybe you have already embarked on some changes. Maybe you are still hesitating at the starting block. That's okay.

Here are the most common challenges you might face when you start using the behaviour principle and how to deal with them.

I am trying but it's too difficult

Acting counter to emotion traps is supposed to feel strange and uncomfortable. Just like weight training, the resistance is a sign that you are working and developing. But it shouldn't be too difficult. If you go too hard you will probably give up before long; you will have a better chance of success if you start with the smallest weights and add heavier weights as you go along.

- **Lower the bar.** What small progress would still be significant for you? Start with a behaviour that you know you can manage. When treating arachnophobia, we don't necessarily start with a live spider encounter – for some, just hearing the word 'spider' or seeing a picture is enough to make the hairs on the back of their neck stand on end. Take it from there.

- **Use training wheels.** I have talked a lot about the importance of avoiding safety behaviours and other crutches that weaken the effect of the behaviour principle, but sometimes you might have to cheat a little just to get started. Would it be easier to start exercising if your friend was with you? Could that difficult phone call be a text message instead?

- **Increase your resilience.** We all have periods when we are more or less sensitive to stress. You can increase your resilience by eating regularly, trying to get enough sleep and being physically active. Schedule behavioural exercises at times when you usually feel alert and strong.

I am too impulsive

You might agree with every word in this book – in theory. But as soon as your emotions kick in, life becomes a battlefield of jealousy, anxiety and emotional outbursts. Perhaps you feel like you don't you get a microsecond's chance to stop your impulses.

If you have problems with impulse control, I can heartily recommend mindfulness training. I know, it's hard – the practice is hardest when the need is greatest. If you have major problems, you can turn to professionals for help.

It is normal to be overwhelmed by strong emotions sometimes. Remember to be compassionate with yourself – you are doing the best you can. Keep going! If you continue to practise in easier situations, you will soon be able to take on the bigger challenges as well.

I can't get started

I suspect the reason you picked up this book to begin with is because you have a pattern of behaviour that you want to change. Now you've ploughed through from cover to cover but are yet to begin in practice. What next?

- **Start with something fun.** Start with changes that sound genuinely appealing. If you want to find an attractive alternative to scrolling on your phone all evening, picking up a literary mammoth à la *War and Peace* is not a good start. Why not start with a juicy thriller or a trip to the cinema?

- **Adjust the thresholds.** Make it easy to do the right thing! Lower the thresholds for desired behaviours, for example by booking yourself onto a course. At the same time, raise the thresholds for unwanted behaviours, for example by tidying distractions away or loudly declaring to everyone around you what you intend to stop doing.

- **Take a moment to think.** You also have to ask yourself: do I really want to change? Which brings us to the next point.

Do I really want this?

Just because you have a tool doesn't mean you are obliged to use it. There can be advantages to ignoring the behaviour principle and continuing in old patterns. In psychotherapy, we talk about secondary gains, i.e. benefits you get from your problems that are rarely obvious at first glance. Maybe you quite like playing the delicate victim and letting your partner be the brave hero who has to chase wasps away for you?

Have a good think about whether the work is worth it. What are you gaining by continuing as you are? What are you missing out on? When you are aware of your genuine motives, it is often easier to make a conscious decision about whether to fight harder or to give up.

I'm trying but it isn't working

Maybe you've tested out the behaviour principle on a number of occasions but it hasn't worked for you. This is usually down to one of the following reasons:

- **You're giving up too quickly.** The absolute most common mistake is to give up when you don't get immediate results. *This method doesn't work for me*, you think. So you leave the party, get out of the lift, call your ex – without giving the method a proper chance. Give your thoughts and feelings some time to catch on. Complete the exercise, preferably on three separate occasions. Only after that can you evaluate.

- **You forget about subtle behaviours.** Another common mistake is to apply the behaviour principle on the surface but also sneakily engage in emotion traps. Maybe you go to a party but spend the whole time avoiding interaction. How would a person who was comfortable in the situation act?

Start with changes that sound genuinely appealing.

- **You are working on the wrong thing.**
  Unfortunately, the behaviour principle is not
  a universal cure. Maybe you're not being
  oversensitive and your friend really is being
  offensive. Always start with going through
  STOP to understand what the problem is and
  whether the behaviour principle is the right
  solution. If you have an unkind friend, learning
  to put up with their insults isn't the solution –
  you need to start standing up for yourself. Also,
  don't forget that some psychological problems
  have medical causes (vitamin D deficiency can
  make you very tired, for example). If you are
  unsure, talk to a health professional.

What if no one likes the new me?

It is common to be assigned a certain role within a
group or relationship, with an unspoken expectation
that you will wear that mantle indefinitely. Change
can cause turmoil when roles suddenly shift. Maybe
people will say you're boring if you stop staying in the
pub until closing time. Maybe your family will wonder
what has got into you when you suddenly start learning
aerial acrobatics.

If the changes aren't too dramatic, you will usually
settle into new roles after a while. The adjustment might
be tough but your friendships probably have a deeper
foundation than just drinking shots together.

And if not, then you have to ask whether the relationship is worth it. Are you willing to give up something that you want in order to preserve the relationship? Sometimes the answer is yes. Sometimes the solution is to go your separate ways.

It's just too much

This book is not a substitute for therapy. I'm afraid self-help books are unlikely to solve all your problems if you are suffering deeply and/or have difficulty functioning in everyday life. Contact a doctor or therapist. They can help you and advise you on what further support is available to you. I wish you the best of luck!

Not allowing for setbacks

Strange though it may sound, psychologists usually look favourably on their client having setbacks at some point during their treatment. Setbacks tend to be extremely illuminating.

Life is constantly changing. Conflicts, job changes, illnesses and crises . . . Sometimes you fall back into old patterns. But these setbacks are excellent opportunities to review your strategy and improve it for the future.

Then there's the 'what-the-hell' effect. This is when you throw up your hands and quit at the slightest setback – and indulge in negative behaviour all the more. The problem here is your reaction, not the setback itself.

When you suffer a setback, pause and think. Answer the following questions, preferably in writing:

- What factors led to the setback? The environment you were in, something that triggered you, a certain person?

- How could you prevent the same thing from happening again?

- If you were about to make the same mistake again, what would the early warning signs be?

- If you notice these warning signs, what should you do to avoid falling at the same hurdle again?

Final Thoughts

I wrote this book for you. And for myself, and your next-door neighbour, and all the millions of people out there who sometimes cry in the shower, doubt themselves or fret their way through life's obstacle course.

Life gives us hard knocks, and so do our emotions. Before your time on earth is done, you will have suffered feelings of jealousy, anger and contempt many times. And I'm sorry to say that you probably haven't seen the last of anxiety, disgust or despair either.

But emotions can also be magnificent. You will have moments of belonging, strength and courage. Not to mention wonder, euphoria and precious moments of profound peace. If you want, you can learn to elicit more of these emotions. And do what you can to make the more difficult feelings as infrequent, mild and short-lived as possible.

Thoughts and feelings follow you through life. They are companions who scout, interpret and call you to action. Sometimes they can appear as your worst enemies. They will try to persuade you to stay on well-trodden paths, eat your packed lunch before lunchtime or wander into the darkest caves where the way out is difficult to find.

They can come across as traitors but in reality, your thoughts and feelings are your staunchest allies. Even if they are quite thoughtless ones – what would you do in that dark cave? Despite their flaws, they are faithful friends who always have your best interests at heart so listen to what they have to say. Allow yourself to get swept away with their enthusiasm sometimes and explore new paths, but when your thoughts and feelings stubbornly stop and point in the wrong direction, don't follow! They may be adamant but you are the one who is holding the map and ultimately knows where you are going. Give them a reassuring smile and walk in the opposite direction, towards your chosen destination. You will find that they shrug their shoulders and tag along surprisingly often.

When your thoughts and feelings stubbornly stop and point in the wrong direction, don't follow!

I don't know which roads you will take. Maybe you want to push the limits to see how far you can go. Tame fear, whip up motivation and conquer every challenge. Live an extraordinary life that will be written about in the history books. Or maybe you want to stay right where you are. To look around exactly where you stand, but with a newfound peace once the chatter of thoughts and emotions has quieted, making the most of now with presence and serenity.

Whichever path you take, I hope you've gained a few tools to help you on your way. This knowledge is too valuable to stay within the four walls of the therapy room. You cannot choose your thoughts and feelings, but you can invite them along new paths and discover how often they accept the invitation.

References

Introduction

Nearly half of participants remembered televised images from Princess Diana's car crash.
Ost, James, et al. 'Crashing memories and reality monitoring: Distinguishing between perceptions, imaginations and "false memories"', *Applied Cognitive Psychology: The Official Journal of the Society for Applied Research in Memory and Cognition* 16.2 (2002): 125–134.

Ninety-seven per cent of all Swedish drivers think they drive as well or better than the average.
'Svenskarna tycker att de är stjärnor bakom ratten' [Swedes think they are experts behind the wheel], *Expressen*, 17 April 2002.

The teacher was perceived as attractive when he was friendly.
Nisbett, Richard E. and Timothy D. Wilson. 'The halo effect: Evidence for unconscious alteration of judgments', *Journal of Personality and Social Psychology* 35.4 (1977): 250.

On self-compassion and its connection to wellbeing.
Zessin, Ulli, Oliver Dickhäuser and Sven Garbade. 'The relationship between self-compassion and wellbeing: A meta-analysis', *Applied Psychology: Health and Well-Being* 7.3 (2015): 340–364.

Self-compassion helps to reduce anxiety, depression and stress, and increases self-care behaviour.
Misurya, Ishita, Pranati Misurya and Anirban Dutta. 'The effect of self-compassion on psychosocial and clinical outcomes in patients with medical conditions: A systematic review', *Cureus* 12.10 (2020).

Self-compassion helps to reduce eating disorders and negative body image.
Braun, Tosca D., Crystal L. Park and Amy Gorin. 'Self-compassion, body image, and disordered eating: A review of the literature', *Body Image* 17 (2016): 117–131.

Self-compassion reduces self-criticism.
Wakelin, Katherine E., Gemma Perman and Laura M. Simonds. 'Effectiveness of self-compassion-related interventions for reducing self-criticism: A systematic review and meta-analysis', *Clinical Psychology & Psychotherapy* (2021).

1. The Self-Esteem Myth

On self-esteem and how it develops over a lifetime.
Orth, Ulrich, Ruth Yasemin Erol and Eva C. Luciano. 'Development of self-esteem from age 4 to 94 years: A meta-analysis of longitudinal studies', *Psychological Bulletin* 144.10 (2018): 1045.

Everyone has a 'performance-based self-esteem' in the sense that self-esteem varies based on how things are going in important areas of life.
Crocker, Jennifer and Connie T. Wolfe. 'Contingencies of self-worth', *Psychological Review* 108.3 (2001): 593.

Rosenberg Self-Esteem Scale
Rosenberg, Morris, 1989. *Society and the Adolescent Self-Image*, Revised edition. Middletown, CT: Wesleyan University Press.

On imposter syndrome.
Bravata, Dena M., et al. 'Prevalence, predictors, and treatment of impostor syndrome: a systematic review', *Journal of General Internal Medicine* 35.4 (2020): 1252–1275.

The study that ended the self-esteem movement.
Baumeister, Roy F. et al. 'Does high self-esteem cause better performance, interpersonal success, happiness, or healthier lifestyles?', *Psychological Science in the Public Interest* 4.1 (2003): 1–44.

Self-esteem grows out of healthy relationships (especially romantic relationships) and vice versa.
Harris, Michelle A. and Ulrich Orth. 'The link between self-esteem and social relationships: A meta-analysis of longitudinal studies', *Journal of Personality and Social Psychology* 119.6 (2020): 1459.

2 . Schedule in Joy

Positive emotions broaden our cognitive and behavioural repertoire.
Fredrickson, Barbara. 'The role of positive emotions in positive psychology: The broaden-and-build theory of positive emotions', *American Psychologist* 56.3 (2001): 218–26.

Depression is characterised by negative thought patterns.
Gotlib, Ian H. and Jutta Joormann. 'Cognition and depression: current status and future directions', *Annual Review of Clinical Psychology* vol. 6 (2010): 285–312.

Depression affects one in three women and one in five men in their lifetime.
Dattani Seloni, 'What is the Lifetime Risk of Depression?', *Our World in Data*, 18 May 2022.

On brooding and worry.
Nolen-Hoeksema, Susan, et al. 'Rethinking Rumination', *Perspectives on Psychological Science: A Journal of the Association for Psychological Science* vol. 3.5 (2008): 400–24.

3 . Stop Waiting for Motivation

On motivation.
Ryan, Richard M. and Edward L. Deci. 'Overview of self-determination theory: An organismic dialectical perspective', *Handbook of Self-determination Research 2* (2002): 3–33.

We perform at our best with a combination of intrinsic and extrinsic motivation.
Cerasoli, Christopher P., Jessica M. Nicklin and Michael T. Ford. 'Intrinsic motivation and extrinsic incentives jointly predict performance: a 40-year meta-analysis', *Psychological Bulletin* 140.4 (2014): 980.

On goal setting.
Locke, Edwin A. and Gary P. Latham. 'New directions in goal-setting theory', *Current Directions in Psychological Science* 15.5 (2006): 265–268.

If you are starting something new, learning goals are often better than performance goals.
Seijts, Gerard H. and Gary P. Latham. 'Learning versus performance goals: When should each be used?' *Academy of Management Perspectives* 19.1 (2005): 124–131.

Gaming in the UK.
'Gaming penetration in the United Kingdom (UK) from 2013 to 2022, by age group and gender', *Statista*, 22 May 2023.

We perform better when our tasks are clear, we feel equipped and get feedback on our progress.
Stajkovic, Alexander D. and Fred Luthans. 'Self-efficacy and work-related performance: A meta-analysis', *Psychological Bulletin* 124.2 (1998): 240.

Feedback increases achievement of goals.
Locke, Edwin A. and Gary P. Latham. 'Building a practically useful theory of goal setting and task motivation: A 35-year odyssey', *American Psychologist* 57.9 (2002): 705.

On negative feedback.
Fong, Carlton J., et al. 'A meta-analysis of negative feedback on intrinsic motivation', *Educational Psychology Review* (2019): 121–162.

The Hunger Games audiobook increases gym attendance.
Milkman, Katherine L., Julia A. Minson and Kevin G.M. Volpp. 'Holding the hunger games hostage at the gym: An evaluation of temptation bundling', *Management Science* 60.2 (2014): 283–299.

Intrinsic motivation makes us exercise more.
Teixeira, Pedro J., et al. 'Exercise, physical activity, and self-determination theory: a systematic review', *International Journal of Behavioral Nutrition and Physical Activity* 9.1 (2012): 1–30.

4 . How to Reduce Worry and Anxiety

Single-session treatments for specific phobia.
Davis, Thompson Elder, Thomas H. Ollendick and Lars-Göran Öst. *Intensive one-session treatment of specific phobias*, New York: Springer, 2012.

On anxiety.
Barlow, David H., ed. *Clinical Handbook of Psychological Disorders: A step-by-step treatment manual*, Guilford Publications, 2021.

On worry.
Borkovec, T.D., William J. Ray and Joachim Stober. 'Worry: A cognitive phenomenon intimately linked to affective, physiological, and interpersonal behavioral processes', *Cognitive Therapy and Research* 22.6 (1998): 561–576.

How anxiety affects thoughts.
Mathews, Andrew. 'Why worry? The cognitive function of anxiety', *Behaviour Research and Therapy* 28.6 (1990): 455–468.

5. On Stress – Work Smarter, Not Harder

Stress can cause physical problems.
Nixon, Ashley E., et al. 'Can work make you sick? A meta-analysis of the relationships between job stressors and physical symptoms', *Work & Stress* 25.1 (2011): 1–22.

Stress increases the risk of getting a cold.
Pedersen, Anette, Robert Zachariae and Dana H. Bovbjerg. 'Influence of psychological stress on upper respiratory infection – a meta-analysis of prospective studies', *Psychosomatic Medicine* 72.8 (2010): 823–832.

Breaks do not impair productivity.
Waongenngarm, Pooriput, Kantheera Areerak and Prawit Janwantanakul. 'The effects of breaks on low back pain, discomfort, and work productivity in office workers: A systematic review of randomized and non-randomized controlled trials', *Applied Ergonomics* 68 (2018): 230–239.

Study that many would rather choose electric shocks than idleness.
Wilson, Timothy D., et al. 'Just think: The challenges of the disengaged mind', *Science* 345.6192 (2014): 75–77.

Active coping.
'Active coping', *APA Dictionary of Psychology*. Retrieved 24 July 2023.

Passive coping.
'Passive coping', *APA Dictionary of Psychology*. Retrieved 24 July 2023.

Multitasking takes mental energy.
Kim, Chobok, et al. 'Domain general and domain preferential brain regions associated with different types of task switching: A meta-analysis', *Human Brain Mapping* 33.1 (2012): 130–142.

Checking emails less often reduces stress.
Kushlev, Kostadin and Elizabeth W. Dunn. 'Checking email less frequently reduces stress', *Computers in Human Behavior* 43 (2015): 220–228.

Team debrief increases productivity.
Tannenbaum, Scott I. and Christopher P. Cerasoli. 'Do team and individual debriefs enhance performance? A meta-analysis', *Human factors* 55.1 (2013): 231–245.

Disconnecting from work in your spare time protects against stress.
Sonnentag, Sabine, Carmen Binnewies and Eva J. Mojza. 'Staying well and engaged when demands are high: The role of psychological detachment', *Journal of Applied Psychology* 95.5 (2010): 965.

The best moods arise from being committed to work during work hours and disconnected in free time.
Sonnentag, Sabine, et al. 'Being engaged at work and detached at home: A week-level study on work engagement, psychological detachment, and affect', *Work & Stress* 22.3 (2008): 257–276.

Conflicts between work and the rest of life increase the risk of exhaustion.
Reichl, Corinna, Michael P. Leiter and Frank M. Spinath. 'Work-nonwork conflict and burnout: A meta-analysis', *Human Relations* 67.8 (2014): 979–1005.

Using work technology in your spare time makes it difficult to disconnect in free time.
Sandoval-Reyes, Juan, Julio C. Acosta-Prado and Carlos Sanchís-Pedregosa. 'Relationship amongst technology use, work overload, and psychological detachment from work', *International Journal of Environmental Research and Public Health* 16.23 (2019): 4602.

The importance of recovery after work.
Bennett, Andrew A., Arnold B. Bakker and James G. Field. 'Recovery from work-related effort: A meta-analysis', *Journal of Organizational Behavior* 39.3 (2018): 262–275.

Physical activity can protect against stress.
Mücke, Manuel, et al. 'Influence of regular physical activity and fitness on stress reactivity as measured with the trier social stress test protocol: A systematic review', *Sports Medicine* 48.11 (2018): 2607–2622.

Exercise in free time increases wellbeing.
Buecker, Susanne, et al. 'Physical activity and subjective wellbeing in healthy individuals: a meta-analytic review', *Health Psychology Review* (2020): 1–19.

Cardio training helps you relax.
Hamer, Mark, Adrian Taylor and Andrew Steptoe. 'The effect of acute aerobic exercise on stress-related blood pressure responses: a systematic review and meta-analysis', *Biological Psychology* 71.2 (2006): 183–190.

Long-term study of 40 American researchers.
Root-Bernstein, Robert S., Maurine Bernstein and Helen Garnier. 'Correlations between avocations, scientific style, work habits, and professional impact of scientists', *Creativity Research Journal* 8.2 (1995): 115–137.

Sleep problems increase the risk of burnout.
Söderström, Marie, et al. 'Insufficient sleep predicts clinical burnout', *Journal of Occupational Health Psychology* 17.2 (2012): 175.

Adults need 7–9 hours of sleep.
Consensus Conference Panel. 'Recommended amount of sleep for a healthy adult: a joint consensus statement of the American Academy of Sleep Medicine and Sleep Research Society', *Journal of Clinical Sleep Medicine* 11.6 (2015): 591–592.

Coffee half-life.
Benowitz, Neal L. 'Clinical pharmacology of caffeine', *Annual Review of Medicine* 41.1 (1990): 277–288.

Rosenberg's Self-Esteem Scale

Here are ten statements about how you feel about yourself. Tick the box that best suits you. When you have answered all the statements, add up the points in the boxes you have ticked. You can calculate your score on the next page.

		Strongly Agree	Agree	Disagree	Strongly Disagree
1.	I feel that I am a person of worth, at least on an equal plane with others.	3	2	1	0
2.	I feel that I have a number of good qualities.	3	2	1	0
3.	All in all, I am inclined to feel that I am a failure.	0	1	2	3

		Strongly Agree	Agree	Disagree	Strongly Disagree
4.	I am able to do things as well as most other people.	3	2	1	0
5.	I feel I do not have much to be proud of.	0	1	2	3
6.	I take a positive attitude towards myself.	3	2	1	0
7.	On the whole, I am satisfied with myself.	3	2	1	0
8.	I wish I could have more respect for myself.	0	1	2	3
9.	I certainly feel useless at times.	0	1	2	3
10.	At times I think I am no good at all.	0	1	2	3

Results of the self-esteem questionnaire

0–15 points: low self-esteem
15–25 points: average self-esteem
25–30 points: high self-esteem

Acknowledgements

The most important insights and tools in this book are not mine – they are repackaged CBT and all I have done is chosen the wrapping paper and tied the bow. All credit goes to the eminent lecturers, authors, researchers, colleagues and supervisors who patiently take all the green psychology students under their wing and train them into fully fledged psychologists. Thank you! Your research and clinical skills save lives.

Warmest thanks to my clients. The courage, perseverance and strength you show week after week, even when life is at its most difficult, never ceases to amaze me. It is a true privilege to be a part of your process. The proudest moments of my life are when we high five over your completed homework. I agree – lifts can be unpleasant. Writers want to do their subject justice and I am so grateful to all the experts who took time out of their world-leading research and clinical practice to read and comment on this manuscript. Thank you to Sweden's most inspiring CBT lecturer Jonas Ramnerö (introduction); the sharp and resourceful Magnus Lindwall (self-esteem); productivity personified Gerhard Andersson (joy); Alexander Rozental (motivation), whose Swedish book on procrastination *Dancing on the Deadline* I cannot recommend highly enough; Per Carlbring (anxiety), who, despite an impressive research career, always manages to respond swiftly to emails; Kerstin Jeding (stress), who is the very definition of warmth and wisdom; Sweden's gift to research into working life Kristin Öster (stress) and the champion of meta-research Gustav Nilsonne (sleep).

A special thanks to my former supervisor Linnea Kollberg and psychologist Liv Svirsky for their support and encouragement when this book idea was still only a small seed. One day, I hope to become as skilled a psychologist as you both.

For their faith and feedback, I would like to thank my brilliant publisher Cecilia Viklund and editor Liselott Wennborg Ramberg. You are proof that writing is best done as a team effort. Thanks also to all the other stars at Bonnier Fakta: Per Lilja, Eva Lindeberg, Sofia Heurlin, Magdalena Höglund and Elena Bozinova for helping to share this knowledge with more people. My deepest gratitude to the team at Lagom. Writing this book, I couldn't dream that it would one day be published in the UK. A special thanks to my translator Annie Prime for heroically protecting my quirks from getting lost in translation, and my publisher Michelle Signore for believing in this book.

This book was written during a global pandemic, during which I clung to the lessons in the chapter on joy to get through with my health intact. Thanks to Neurora, the book club and Salongen, who followed the process, cheered me on and – above all – gave me meaning and energy for life.

About The Author

Siri Helle is a licensed psychologist and has worked with CBT-treatment for depression, stress and anxiety. She recently worked with thirty renowned NGOs in Sweden to make mental health part of the school curriculum and regularly appears as a psychological expert in Swedish medias. She was the winner of the Psychology Student of the Year Award in 2017 for popularising psychological knowledge. As a public speaker and science communicator, Helle is an appreciated expert in Swedish business and media. *The Emotion Trap* is her first book to be translated into English; it was first published in March 2022 in Sweden and has been a bestseller.

Index